Contents

Jigs barked as if to say, "Oh boy!"

Then Shea heard a strange laughing noise. It seemed to be coming from behind the big oak tree. The tree stood in the middle of the field.

Shea told Jigs, "Keep quiet. Don't make a sound."

They sneaked ever so quietly toward the big oak. The laughter got louder and louder. Shea peeked around the tree trunk. She couldn't believe it! Right before her very eyes was a tiny man. He was dressed all in green. He was dancing and singing a happy song.

Come along, me dear lassie,
Oh, come along quick.
This wee Irishman is
playing his old tricks.

Come along, me dear lassie,
Oh, come find me gold,
Before the day passes
and I grow another year old.

After You Read

Practice the leprechaun's poem.
Can you sound like a leprechaun as you read it?
When you are ready, read it to an adult.

Shea jumped from behind the tree. She grabbed the little leprechaun by his sleeve. Then she shouted, "Give me your gold!"

"So! Ye got me, little lass!" the leprechaun replied. "Just let go of me jacket sleeve. Then I will tell ye where to find me bag of gold."

Without thinking, Shea did as she was told. To her surprise the leprechaun did not run away. Instead, the wee man said, "Go to the big rock in the center of the buttercup patch. Look all around. 'Tis there ye shall find me bag of gold."

Shea rushed to the buttercup patch as fast as she could. Jigs followed at her heels. She searched everywhere for the leprechaun's bag of gold. All she found was petals, petals, and more petals.

Shea hurried back to where she had caught the leprechaun. Of course he had disappeared. All that was left behind was a small four-leaf clover.

Shea picked up the four-leaf clover. Sadly, she looked back toward the buttercup patch. There was that tricky leprechaun dancing a jig on the big rock. He was holding his bag of gold and laughing merrily.

"Happy St. Patrick's Day! Better luck next year!" the crafty leprechaun shouted. And with that, he was gone!

All the way home Shea thought about that clever leprechaun. She thought about how she had let him get away. She thought about his bag of gold.

"Next year I won't let go of that leprechaun," she told Jigs. "I'll make him give me his bag of gold."

Jigs answered with a happy bark.

"Come on, Jigs!" said Shea smiling. "Wait 'til Mom and Dad hear this story!"

Questions about
Shea and the Leprechaun

1. What did Shea plan to do on Saint Patrick's Day?

   ○ go to a Saint Patrick's Day parade
   ○ go to a leprechaun's party
   ○ go out and catch a leprechaun

2. How did Shea catch the leprechaun?

   ○ She caught the leprechaun in a trap.
   ○ She grabbed the leprechaun's sleeve.
   ○ Her dog caught the leprechaun.

3. Why do you suppose the leprechaun didn't run away when Shea let go of his sleeve?

   _____

   _____

4. How did the leprechaun trick Shea?

   _____

   _____

5. What do you think Shea might do next year?

   _____

   _____

6. Do you think Shea's mom and dad will believe her when she tells them her story? Why or why not?

   _____

   _____

   _____

Tell It in Order

A. Number these events in the order in which they happened in the story.

_____ Shea grabbed the leprechaun by his sleeve.

_____ The tricky leprechaun was dancing on the rock.

_____ She searched everywhere for the bag of gold.

_____ He yelled, "Better luck next year!"

_____ The leprechaun told Shea the gold was by the big
rock in the buttercup patch.

_____ Shea said, "Next year I won't let go of that leprechaun."

- -

B. Use the information from the story to answer these questions.

1. What did Shea do first when she got out of bed?

_____

_____

2. What did Shea do after the leprechaun was gone?

_____

_____

_____

What Does It Mean?

A. Write the letter of each underlined word on the line in front of its meaning.

1. The <u>meadow</u> was filled with flowers.

   a

2. The two <u>companions</u> sneaked closer to the big oak tree.

   b

3. Come along, me dear <u>lassie</u>.

   c

4. She looked all around and found nothing but <u>petals</u>.

   d

5. The leprechaun was dancing a <u>jig</u>.

   e

6. The <u>crafty</u> little man disappeared.

   f

_____ the colorful parts of flowers

_____ a young girl

_____ a fast dance

_____ an area of grassy ground

_____ skilled at tricking others

_____ close friends

B. Circle the words that describe the leprechaun in the story.

clever	large	sneaky	slow	witty	unlucky
old	foolish	smart	mean	fluffy	tricky

Compound Words

A **compound word** is two smaller words put together to make one new word. Use the words in the box to make compound words.

butter	rain	every	walk	sun	time
spring	light	cup	bow	where	side

1. _____   4. _____

2. _____   5. _____

3. _____   6. _____

Draw a picture of each compound word below.

buttercup	rainbow
sunlight	butterfly

Words That Describe

Some special words describe things or actions. These words make writing more interesting.

four-leaf	clever	quickly	quietly	yellow
pretty	beautiful	tiny	merrily	

A. Choose the best descriptive word above to complete each sentence.

1. Shea saw a _____ man dancing by the tree.

2. She picked up the _____ clover.

3. The leprechaun _____ disappeared.

4. That _____ leprechaun had tricked them again.

5. The _____ buttercups smelled sweet.

6. They tiptoed _____ through the meadow.

7. It was a _____ day to catch a leprechaun.

8. The leprechaun laughed _____ as he held his bag of gold.

B. Write a sentence using two words from the list above.

_____

_____

Crossword Fun

Word Box

Shea	leprechaun	Jigs	meadows	buttercup
lassie	yellow	St. Patrick	sunshine	lucky

Across

4. _____ and the Leprechaun
5. a tiny make-believe man
6. Shea's dog
7. a yellow flower
8. having good luck

Down

1. a young girl
2. a saint
3. grassy grounds
4. sunlight
9. color of buttercups

Owls

It is a dark, clear night. Strange sounds come through the trees. "Whooo! Whooo!" A great horned owl is awake. He is perched high above the forest floor. His large round eyes scan the ground. He is looking for something to eat. Suddenly he is in the air. Silently he glides toward his prey. The unaware mouse is busily gathering seeds. In one swift movement, the great owl grabs the rodent with his sharp claws. He carries it back to his perch. There he eats his first meal of the night.

Many people have never seen or heard an owl in the wild. This is because most owls are nocturnal, or night animals. They rarely move around during the day. They are at home everywhere but Antarctica. Owls live in forests, deserts, meadows, and even in swamps. Some owls have learned to live with people. They live in such places as barns and old buildings.

There are over 130 different kinds of owls around the world. Eighteen types of owls live in North America. Most owls are gray or brown. Lighter and darker feathers form patterns on each owl. This helps them blend in with their surroundings. Other owls, like the snowy owl, are white. The white coloring helps this owl hide in snowy areas.

Great Gray Owl

After You Read

Practice reading this page.
Read the numbers carefully.
When you can read the page with
no mistakes, read it to an adult.

The largest North American owl is the great gray owl. This owl has a big face and fluffy feathers. It stands about 30 inches (76 centimeters) tall. It weighs about 3 pounds (1½ kilograms). When this owl takes flight, its wingspan is almost 5 feet (1½ meters) wide. The great gray owl lives in the northern United States. Spruce and fir trees are its favorite homes.

The smallest owl is the elf owl. It is only about 6 inches (15 centimeters) tall and weighs less than one ounce (28 grams). Elf owls live in the southwestern United States. They like warm weather. Elf owls make their homes in giant cactus plants. The holes they use were drilled out by woodpeckers.

Elf Owl

Great Horned Owl

The great horned owl is the fiercest of all owls. It is sometimes called "the feathered tiger of the air."

Many owls have tufts of feathers, sometimes called horns, on the top of their heads. These "horns" look like ears, but they are not. An owl's ears are under the feathers on both sides of its head. An owl's hearing is very keen. Often an owl can find its prey by sound alone.

Owls have more feathers than most birds. Their fluffy feathers make them look larger than they are. When an owl is in danger, it will "puff" up its feathers. Then the owl looks even bigger. It will try to frighten away an enemy in this way.

Owls are predators. They hunt at night for small animals such as rats, mice, and insects. Larger owls eat skunks, rabbits, and sometimes other birds. Farmers like owls because they eat the animals that harm their crops. An owl can eat three or four rodents a night.

Owls have fringed feathers on the edges of their wings. These make the owl's flight silent. A mouse or rabbit won't even know the owl is near until it strikes.

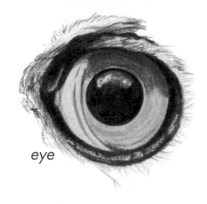

eye

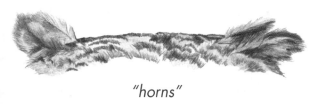

talons

"horns"

owl feather

Owls are easily recognized by their large yellow or orange eyes. Their eyes help them hunt at night. An owl's eyes point forward the same way ours do. But owls can't move their eyes from side to side. They must turn their heads to see to the side. Some owls can turn their heads almost all the way around.

Owls catch their prey with their powerful talons, or claws. Then the owl will take it to a nearby tree to feed. Owls use their sharp beaks to tear the food. The flesh of the animal is digested. The bones, feathers, and teeth are pressed into a ball called a pellet. This pellet is pushed out of the owl's mouth. It is left somewhere on the forest floor. If you are walking in the woods, you might find owl pellets on the ground. Look around. An owl is nearby.

People have always been fascinated by owls. In stories they are often called "the wise owl." This may be because their large eyes give them a human look. In truth, owls are not the smartest of all birds. But they are very helpful to our environment. Like all birds of prey, owls are protected by law. It is against the law for anyone to harm an owl.

Questions about
Owls

1. Why have many people never seen or heard an owl in the wild?

○ Owls don't make a sound.

○ Owls hide from people.

○ Owls are nocturnal.

2. Name four places where owls live.

_____

_____

3. Why must owls turn their heads from side to side?

_____

4. Which of these is NOT food for an owl?

○ mice   ○ seeds   ○ insects

5. What is an owl pellet?

_____

_____

6. How do farmers feel about owls? Why?

_____

_____

_____

7. Why are owls protected by law?

_____

_____

_____

Tell It in Order

A. On the lines below, explain how an owl hunts for food. The first statement has been done for you.

First, an owl swoops down on its prey.

Next,

_____

_____

Then,

_____

Last,

_____

~~~~~~

B. Number these sentences in the order in which they happened in the story.

_____ Silently he glides toward a mouse.

_____ There he quickly eats his first meal of the night.

_____ A great horned owl is awake.

_____ The great owl grabs the rodent with his talons.

_____ His round eyes scan the ground, looking for food.

_____ He carries it back to his perch.

What Does It Mean?

Use the Word Box to find the correct meaning for each vocabulary word. Then circle each word in the word search.

Word Box

rodent	talons	prey	digest
perch	pellet	predator	nocturnal

1. a small ball

_____

2. an animal hunted for food

_____

3. happening at night

_____

4. a place to rest or sit

_____

5. the claws of a bird

_____

6. a small mammal

_____

7. to break down food

_____

8. an animal that hunts

_____

```
P R E Y U D H D F J
X O K S C A N I E S
Z D Q O W L S G B P
P E V P E L L E T E
G N I N N A C S L R
I T A L O N S T W C
N O C T U R N A L H
S L P R E D A T O R
```

Prefixes

A **prefix** is a word part that is added to the beginning of a base word. A prefix changes the meaning of the word.

Here are three prefixes and their meanings:

| mis = bad or wrong | re = again | dis = not or opposite |

A. Add a prefix to each base word.

1. _____like

2. _____place

3. _____plant

4. _____take

5. _____new

6. _____write

7. _____trust

8. _____think

9. _____grace

10. _____spell

B. Choose words from the list above to complete each sentence.

1. Don't _____ the tufts of feathers on an owl for horns.

2. Farmers _____ rodents in their fields.

3. At school we will _____ our story about owls.

4. The farmer must _____ his wheat fields.

C. Write a sentence of your own using a word from the list above.

_____

_____

Alphabetical Order

Write the names of these owls in alphabetical order on the lines below.

snowy owl	great horned owl	elf owl	burrowing owl
screech owl	gray owl	barn owl	dwarf owl
spotted owl	barking owl	eagle owl	
pygmy owl	barred owl	spectacled owl	

1. barking owl

2. _____ owl

3. barred owl

4. _____ owl

5. _____ owl

6. _____ owl

7. _____ owl

8. _____ owl

9. great horned owl

10. _____ owl

11. _____ owl

12. _____ owl

13. spectacled owl

14. _____ owl

Whooo's Talking?

Put **quotation marks** where they belong. The first one has been done for you.

1. The boy yelled, "Look at that beautiful owl!"

2. An elf owl screeched, I am the smallest owl!

3. A little girl asked, Are all owls brown?

4. The farmer said, It is nice to have owls eat the mice.

5. A great horned owl screamed, I am the fiercest of all owls!

Alike and Different

Think about what you learned about great gray owls and elf owls.
How are they alike? How are they different?
Write at least three facts in each space of the diagram.

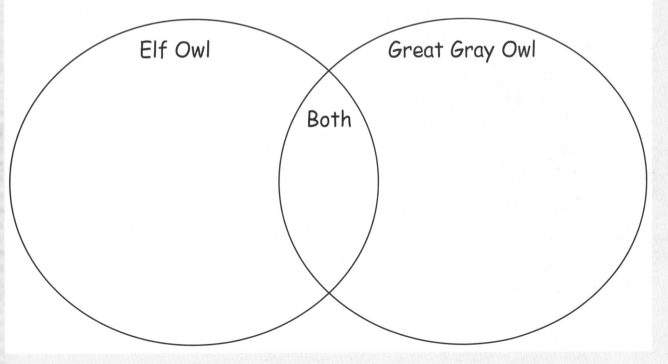

Elf Owl   Both   Great Gray Owl

A New School Day

My room slowly lightens, things start to appear.
Busy neighborhood sounds soon reach my ear.

Dogs sound out with loud, joyful barks.
Birds trill morning songs. I think they are larks.

I rise from my bed to begin the day.
I dress, have breakfast, then I'm on my way.

At the corner my friends and I wait for our bus.
We get on right away; there's never a fuss.

Our school's up ahead, the flag's in our sight.
In we go to read, do numbers, and write.

I find my desk, my class has begun.
I'm glad to be here—learning is fun!

After You Read

Practice reading the poem. The sentences are long.
It will help if you read the phrases in each line carefully.
When you are ready, read the poem to an adult.

Questions about
A New School Day

1. Explain why the author says "things start to appear."

_____

_____

2. What other sounds from the neighborhood might the author have heard?

_____

_____

3. How does the author feel about going to school? How do you know?

_____

_____

_____

4. Do you feel the same way as the author? Explain your answer.

_____

_____

_____

_____

Rhyming Words

Read the poem again. Write the word in the poem that rhymes
with each word below.

1. sight _____   4. fun _____

2. day _____   5. bus _____

3. ear_____   6. barks _____

Word Families

Think of rhyming words for each of the word families below.

un	ight
_____	_____
_____	_____
_____	_____

ay	ear
_____	_____
_____	_____
_____	_____

Animals in Winter

Winter can be a hard time for animals. The weather may be wet and cold. Food can be hard to find under the snow. But nature has given animals different ways to survive. Let's look at how animals make it through this season.

Animals survive during winter in four main ways. Some animals get fat in the fall. They eat and eat and eat. Their bodies store the food as fat. Other animals store fresh food for the cold days ahead. Many animals sleep through the winter months. Still other animals move south. Here the weather is warmer and there is fresh food to eat.

Moose store food in their bodies as fat. The deep snow makes it difficult for them to find food. Their bodies use the stored fat for energy. The layer of fat keeps them warm, too. Moose will also grow heavy coats of hair as the days become colder. This thick hair will warm them like our winter coats, mittens, and hats warm us. Bighorn sheep, deer, buffalo, and antelope are other animals that store food in their bodies.

Many animals that live in dens and burrows store fresh food to eat. They stay inside and sleep much of the winter. Prairie dogs, chipmunks, and beavers are three such animals. They don't really hibernate. On warmer winter days, they wake and eat some of the stored food. They may lie in the sun to soak up its warmth. As soon as the temperature starts dropping, they move into their shelters. Then they go back to sleep.

Hibernators are animals that sleep all winter long. They don't eat at all. Before winter these animals eat and eat and eat to get fat. When winter comes, they curl up and go to sleep. Their hearts beat very slowly. Their body temperature drops. In this way they don't use much of the fat stored in their bodies. Snakes, bears, turtles, and bats all hibernate.

Some animals will leave cold places. They move south. Here the weather is warmer and food is easier to find. This is called migrating.

Many birds fly south. In the fall they gather in large groups. Together they will make the journey. In the spring when the temperature rises, they will return.

Questions about
Animals in Winter

1. Name the four important ways animals survive during the winter.

_____

_____

_____

_____

2. How does an extra layer of fat help the moose?

_____

_____

3. **Hibernators** are animals that _____.
   - ○ lie in the sun to soak up warmth
   - ○ sleep in a dark place all winter
   - ○ travel to a sunny place

4. What do animals that migrate do?
   - ○ sleep all winter
   - ○ travel to a warm place
   - ○ spend winter in a cold place

5. Name two things that happen to an animal that hibernates.

_____

_____

6. What can a heavy coat of hair on animals be compared to?

_____

_____

Tell It in Order

Below are two sequence maps about **migration** and **hibernation**. Fill in the missing parts of each map by using the information from the story.

Migration is the round-trip journey some animals make from colder areas to warmer areas and back again.

First, the days grow shorter and the weather starts to get colder.

Next, _____

_____

Last, _____

_____

First, _____

_____

Next, their heart beats very slowly and they depend on the energy stored in their bodies.

Hibernation is when an animal spends the winter months sleeping and does not eat.

Last, _____

_____

What Does It Mean?

A. Write the number of each word on the line in front of its meaning.

1. survive   _____ traveling as the seasons change

2. shelter   _____ something that protects or covers

3. energy   _____ a measure of heat

4. burrow   _____ fuel or power

5. hibernate   _____ to sleep through the winter

6. migrating   _____ a trip; travels

7. temperature   _____ to live; last through

8. journey   _____ an underground home

B. Illustrate each word below.

─── hibernate ───	─── migrate ───

Adding er and est

er is often added to the end of a word to compare **two things.**

est is often added to the end of a word to compare **more than two things.**

A. Add **er** and **est** to these words.

1. cold ___colder___ ___coldest___

2. deep _____ _____

3. strong _____ _____

4. long _____ _____

5. short _____ _____

6. fast _____ _____

B. Choose a word from the list above to complete each sentence.

1. That was the _____ math test I've ever taken.
   I didn't think I'd finish in time.

2. When you compare depth, Lake Tahoe is _____
   than Mono Lake.

3. Of the two boys, who is the _____?

4. Keesha is the _____ in the class at doing the
   multiplication facts.

5. I have to write a lot of words. Please give me the _____
   of the two pencils.

Change y to i

A. Change the **y** to an **i** and then add the ending given for each word.

1. body (es) _____

2. try (es) _____

3. busy (ly) _____

4. empty (ed) _____

5. bury (ed) _____

6. easy (ly) _____

■ ■

B. Choose a word from the list above to complete each sentence.

1. The squirrel _____ the acorn to save it for winter.

2. A hungry elk _____ to find food under the deep snow.

3. All of the strongest animals _____ survived the winter.

4. The chipmunk is _____ putting food for the winter in its burrow.

5. Hibernators use the energy stored in their _____ to keep them alive through the cold months.

Sort the Sounds

Circle the letters for the long vowel sound in each word.
Write the word in the correct box.

sleep	eat	season	lie
snake	easy	beaver	toad
doe	tight	shy	paint
able	may	so	blow
night	snow	main	time

long a

long e

long i

long o

Reading • EMC 4531 • © Evan-Moor Corp.

The Proud Turkey

Many years ago there lived a turkey who was proud of his looks. He would stare at himself in the mirror for hours. Then he would brag out loud, "I am the most wonderful and colorful animal around."

Every day he would walk past the other animals. He would show off his feathers and boast. "I am so beautiful. Move out of my way!"

One day Turkey trotted past without saying a word to anyone. This made the animals mad. They thought Turkey was too proud. They wanted him to quit acting better than others. Together they formed a terrific plan.

Porcupine pulled out one of his quills. He dipped it in red berry juice. He scribbled a note inviting Turkey to dinner. Rabbit delivered the invitation. He read it aloud:

> Dear Turkey,
>   You are invited to a special dinner. Please go to Fox's den at sundown. There will be a great feast waiting for you to enjoy. Come looking your very best.
>   All of Us

Turkey was so excited, he hurried Rabbit out the door. Then he began to preen and poof out all of his grand feathers. As the sun went down, Turkey arrived at Fox's door. Turkey looked wonderful.

The animals rolled out a red carpet. Turkey strutted down the carpet. All the animals bowed and cheered. Turkey walked around and showed off his feathers.

Then Mole led Turkey to the dining room. Goose served a fantastic feast. Turkey began stuffing himself.

Just as Turkey was eating the last bite of dessert, a beautiful peacock entered the dining room. Turkey was shocked at such a fine display of feathers. He choked on his tart and became speechless. The only sound he could make was, "Gobble, gobble, gobble." All his friends began to laugh. Turkey was horrified. "I look like a fool," thought Turkey. He waddled out the door as quickly as he could. Away he flew into the woods.

For several days no one saw Turkey. The animals went looking for him, but he was nowhere to be found. Everyone began to feel bad about what they had done. They just wanted to teach Turkey to be more humble. They didn't want to hurt his feelings. What they needed was a new plan. This time they asked the wise owl for help.

The wise owl listened to the story. After some time, he spoke. "Look to the safety of the trees and you will find whoooo you seek!"

"I know where he is!" shouted Squirrel. "Follow me!"

Reading • EMC 4531 • © Evan-Moor Corp.

Deep in the forest stood an old oak tree. Its branches were a good place for a turkey to roost. As the animals approached the old oak, they heard a gobbling sound. It came from high in the tree. The search was over. There sat Turkey. He looked very sad and lonely.

Porcupine began to climb up the tree. Peacock stopped him. He would fly up to Turkey. He would ask Turkey to come down and talk. After all, he had been the one who upset Turkey.

Peacock flew to the branch where Turkey sat. "Your friends are worried about you," said Peacock. "They are sorry for what they did."

Before long the two birds flew to the ground. All the animals gathered around them. "We are sorry for the mean trick we played on you, Turkey," the animals said.

"And I am sorry I was so proud and rude," replied Turkey.

"I think we should have another party!" said the clever fox. Off they headed to Fox's den. They would plan a grand dinner party together.

Moral: *Be proud of your wonderful qualities. But do not think that they make you better than others.*

Questions about
The Proud Turkey

1. How did Turkey feel about himself?

_____

_____

2. How did the other animals feel about Turkey?

_____

_____

3. Think of three words you would use to describe Turkey.

_____   _____   _____

4. Do you think what the other animals did to Turkey was right? Why
   do you think this way?

_____

_____

_____

5. List two things that the other animals did when Turkey arrived
   at Fox's den for dinner.

_____

_____

6. Why do you think the author wrote the story "The Proud Turkey"?

   ○ to give information about a turkey and a peacock
   ○ to tell about beautiful animals in the wild
   ○ to say that we should not think we are better than others
   ○ to show how animals live together in the wilderness

Tell It in Order

Number these events in the order in which they happened in the story.

_____ The turkey choked on a tart.

_____ All the animals invited the turkey to dinner.

_____ A peacock entered the dining room.

_____ The animals asked the wise owl for help.

_____ Every day the turkey would brag about himself.

_____ The porcupine scribbled an invitation to the turkey.

_____ All the animals planned another party with no surprises.

_____ The turkey was roosting in an old oak tree.

_____ The only sound the turkey could make was, "Gobble, gobble, gobble."

_____ The animals thought the turkey was too proud.

What Does It Mean?

Word Box

| preen | rude | roost | humble | horrified | approached |
| clever | brag | mirror | carpet | tart | waddled |

Across

1. showing a quick mind; smart
3. a surface that reflects light
4. moved from side to side when walking
6. shocked; filled with alarm
9. a small pie
10. to clean or trim with the beak

Down

1. rug; fabric floor covering
2. impolite
5. came near to
6. not speaking too highly of oneself
7. a resting place where birds perch
8. to speak with too much pride about oneself

Add an Ending

A. Add *endings* to these words.

er	est

1. kind _____ _____

2. proud _____ _____

3. grand _____ _____

4. quick _____ _____

5. quiet _____ _____

B. Use the words above to complete these sentences.

1. A fox can run _____ than a porcupine.

2. Standing in the middle of a forest is one of the _____ places I know.

3. Saving an owl from dying is one of the things I am

   _____ of.

4. At the beginning of the story, all the other animals were

   _____ than the turkey.

5. At the end of the story, the fox made an even _____ dinner for the turkey.

Word Pyramids

A. Think about the story "The Proud Turkey." Use words from the story to help you create a word pyramid about the turkey.

Follow these directions:

Line 1: Topic (This one has been done for you.)
Line 2: Two words describing the topic
Line 3: Three words that show his actions
Line 4: Four words describing his feelings

Turkey

B. Make your own word pyramid about an animal of your choice.

Making Comparisons

For each statement, make an X in the correct box.

	Peacock	Turkey
Is a bird		
Is raised for food		
Has brilliant blue or green feathers		
Has a large fan-shaped tail		
Was important to the Pilgrims		
Tail is marked with eyelike spots		
Has a wattle on its neck		

The Seabottom Hotel

Your Dream Vacation Spot

The Seabottom Hotel is just the spot for you and your family. This wonderful inn rests on the bottom of the Blue Sea.

Don't miss the sights! See colorful fish, plant life, and rare undersea animals from every window.

There's so much to do at the Seabottom Hotel. That's why it's called "The Most Fun City Anywhere—Land, Sea, or Sky." Ride on the back of a seahorse. Play golf on our Swordfish Golf Course. Learn to swim with the tuna.

The Seabottom Hotel

Swordfish Golf

Ride a Wild Seahorse

Meet the Stars

★ *Get here by submarine.*

★ *Children under 12 stay free.*

★ *No sunscreen needed.*

Come Join Us! Call 1-000-SEA-FISH

NO ONE IS EVER "CRABBY" AT THE SEABOTTOM HOTEL

Reading • EMC 4531 • © Evan-Moor Corp.

Questions about
The Seabottom Hotel

1. Why do you think the hotel is named the Seabottom Hotel?

_____

2. What can be seen from every window?

○ rare undersea animals

○ tall buildings

○ strange and unusual trees

3. What do you get to do with the tuna?

○ eat the tuna

○ catch the tuna

○ swim with the tuna

4. Why do you think no one is ever "crabby" at the hotel?

_____

_____

5. Why is sunscreen not needed when you visit the Seabottom Hotel?

_____

_____

6. How will you get to the hotel?

○ by airplane

○ by ocean liner

○ by submarine

7. Would you like to vacation at the Seabottom Hotel? Tell why or why not.

_____

_____

_____

Nouns

A **noun** is a word that names a **person, place,** or **thing.**

A. Write each noun under the correct heading.

sea star	diver	hotel
seabottom	seahorse	golfer
shell	singer	inn
swordfish	waiter	airport
child	golf course	octopus

Person	Place	Thing
_____	_____	_____
_____	_____	_____
_____	_____	_____
_____	_____	_____
_____	_____	_____

B. Choose one noun from each of the headings above. Then write three sentences using those nouns.

1. _____

2. _____

3. _____

Bats

Many stories have been told about bats. People in Europe once feared bats. Maybe bats were feared because they looked scary. Or maybe it was because they only came out at night. But people in Persia and in China weren't afraid of bats. To them, bats meant good luck, long life, and happiness.

People used to think that bats were birds. Today we know that bats are mammals. They are the only mammals that fly.

Like all mammals, bats are warmblooded. They feed their babies milk. Bats live all over the world, except where it is very cold. Most bats live near the equator. In cooler climates, bats will either hibernate or migrate during the winter.

There are over 900 kinds of bats. Both the largest and the smallest bats live in Asia. The largest bat is the flying fox. It weighs about two pounds. Its wingspan is 6 feet (almost 2 meters). The smallest bat is the size of a bumblebee. It weighs less than a penny. Most bats are just big enough to fit into your hand.

Bats are nocturnal. That means they are active at night. During the day, bats sleep hanging upside down. They sleep in caves, hollow trees, attics, and old buildings. Some bats have even been found roosting in spider webs. Now that can get pretty sticky!

Flying Fox

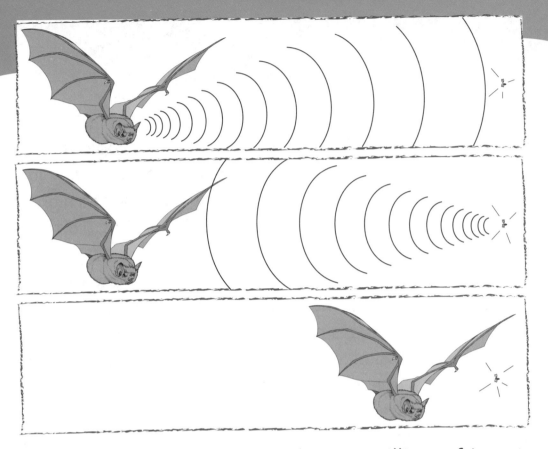

Most bats eat insects. In fact, they eat millions of insects a year. This makes them very helpful to humans. Other bats eat fish, birds, frogs, and small mammals. Some bats eat fruit and drink nectar. These bats often carry their food to their roosts. Along the way they drop seeds. This helps spread plants to new areas.

The vampire bat is perhaps the most famous, but it doesn't attack people. It drinks the blood of some animals. This bat is found only in Mexico and Central and South America.

People once thought that bats were blind. This is not true. Some bats have very good eyesight. But bats use more than seeing to catch their food. Bats, like dolphins, use something called echolocation. A bat makes high-pitched squeaks. The squeaks bounce off nearby objects. As a bat gets closer to something, the echoes bounce back to its ears more quickly. This tells the bat where the thing is, how big it is, and even if it is something good to eat.

A bat's body is covered with fur. Its wings are covered with many fine, leathery hairs. Bats look a bit like a mouse with wings. There are many colors of bats. They can have brown, gray, orange, white, black, or yellow hair. Some bats have red hair. There are even a few bats with white stripes.

Most bats have only one baby, or pup, a year. Pups are born in the spring or early summer. The pups of most insect-eating bats are born with no hair and closed eyes. Some pups can take care of themselves by the time they are three or four weeks old. Others will be able to hunt on their own when four months old. Bats can live for a long time. Some bats have been found that are over thirty years old.

The number of bats has dropped all over the world. Some bats are now extinct. In some places where there used to be thousands, there are now only a few hundred. The habitats of many bats are being destroyed at a very fast rate. Some bats are even being hunted and trapped in their caves. But there is something we can do to help these important mammals. Spread the truth about bats to your friends. Let them know that bats are clean and helpful to have around. They are a very important part of the food chain. Without them, things may get a little "pesty"!

Insect-Eating Bats

Hog-Nosed Bat

Northern Ghost Bat

Fruit-Eating Bats

Greater Fruit Bat

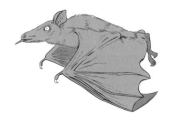

Long-Tongued Bat

Questions about
Bats

1. Name two things people once thought about bats that are not true.

   _____

   _____

2. Name three places where you could look to find a bat.

   _____

   _____

3. Give two reasons why bats are mammals.

   _____

   _____

4. Why has the number of bats declined over the past years?

   _____

   _____

5. Do you think it is important to save bats? Why or why not?

   _____

   _____

   _____

6. Give two facts about bats that you thought were the most interesting.

   _____

   _____

   _____

   _____

Tell It in Order

Number these sentences in the correct order to tell a story about a little brown bat.

_____ It awoke after dark.

_____ At dawn the brown bat returned to its roost.

_____ The bat began searching for something to eat.

_____ A little brown bat slept in the attic of an old building.

_____ All night long it fed on tasty insects.

_____ Then it flew from its roost.

_____ It was tired and ready to sleep once again.

Echolocation

Finish the sentences to tell how bats use echolocation to find food.

First, a bat flies and makes high-pitched squeaks.

Next,

_____

_____

Last,

_____

_____

What Does It Mean?

A. Read the following words and their meanings.

> **extinct**: no longer living
> **roost**: a resting place to perch
> **echolocation**: determining the distance of objects using sound
> **mammals**: animal group in which the females produce milk for their young
> **nocturnal**: active at night
> **pests**: animals that are harmful or troublesome to humans

Use the words above to complete these sentences.

1. Bats are the only _____ that can fly.

2. Some fruit-eating bats _____ in trees.

3. Bats are _____. They are active at night.

4. Bats use _____ to fly at night.

5. Bats help limit the number of harmful _____.

6. Unfortunately, some bats are now _____.

B. Use information from the story to answer these questions.

1. What are the names of three countries named in the story?

_____ _____ _____

2. What are the names of three continents named in the story?

_____ _____ _____

More Than One

Most nouns are made plural by just adding **s**.
Nouns that end in **s**, **ch**, **sh**, or **x** are made plural by adding **es**.

A. Write the plural of each of these nouns by adding **s** or **es**.

1. bat _____   7. cave _____

2. fruit _____   8. frog _____

3. animal _____   9. tree _____

4. human _____   10. moth _____

5. bird _____   11. mammal _____

6. flying fox _____ 12. female _____

B. Choose three of the new words you made above. Use each word in a
question about bats. Remember to use a question mark (**?**).

Example: Did you know that bats are the only **mammals** that fly?

1. _____

_____

2. _____

_____

3. _____

_____

Verbs

Present Tense	Past Tense
happening now	happened in the past
*I like to **watch** bats fly at night.*	*I **watched** a bat fly into the cave.*

A. To make a verb in the past tense, sometimes we just add **ed**.
At other times we must first drop a silent **e** or change **y** to **i**.
Write the missing tense of each verb.

Present Tense		Past Tense
1. _____ feared	1. scare	_____
2. _____ pitched	2. hunt	_____
3. _____ covered	3. hurry	_____
4. _____ tried	4. help	_____
5. _____ walked	5. bounce	_____

B. Some verbs do <u>not</u> add **ed** to make the past tense. The spelling
changes. These are called **irregular verbs**.

Write the number of each present tense word on the line in front of its
past tense form.

1. fly	_____ saw
2. tell	_____ caught
3. hear	_____ took
4. catch	_____ flew
5. feel	_____ grew
6. see	_____ heard
7. grow	_____ felt
8. take	_____ told

More Than One Meaning

Fill in the circle for the correct meaning.

1. In this story, **bat** means _____ .

   ○ a wooden or metal stick used for hitting a ball

   ○ a small flying mammal

   ○ to take a turn trying to hit a ball

2. In this story, **fly** means_____ .

   ○ a small insect

   ○ the flap covering the zipper on a pair of pants

   ○ to travel through the air

3. In this story, **spring** means _____.

   ○ a place where water rises up from underground

   ○ to jump suddenly

   ○ the season between winter and summer

4. In this story, **pound** means _____.

   ○ a unit of weight

   ○ to keep hitting something with force

   ○ a place where stray animals are kept

They Sound the Same

Circle the correct word.

1. The _____ fell all day.   rein   rain

2. The bats _____ back to the cave.   flu   flew

3. The big-eared bat _____ the echo.   heard   herd

4. The bat hung by its _____ as it slept.   feet   feat

Two Groundhog Friends

**"If Candlemas Day is bright and clear,
There will be two winters in the year!"**

Many years ago people believed that if the sun appeared on February 2, known as Candlemas Day, an animal would cast a shadow. This would mean six more weeks of bad weather. Early German immigrants settled in what is now Pennsylvania. Many woodchucks, or groundhogs, lived in this area. The settlers believed that the groundhog was very smart and could predict this kind of information. Thus, people began celebrating Groundhog Day in the United States in the early 1880s, and have ever since! The groundhog became famous overnight!

Once upon a time a young groundhog named Gilbert went scampering across the meadow. He wanted to play with his friend Fred. Fred was a whole year older than Gilbert and knew lots of things about life. That's why Gilbert loved playing with Fred so much.

On this day Gilbert found Fred at the entrance of his burrow, basking in the warm sun. Gilbert talked Fred into running around for little while. As the two friends were playing tag, Fred stopped suddenly and said, "Brrr! I feel chilled. It's getting to be that time again!"

"What time again?" asked Gilbert.

"WINTER! Time for us to go to sleep," replied Fred.

"But I don't want to go to sleep," cried Gilbert.

"You must," said Fred. "The snow will soon fall and cover everything around as far as you can see like a white blanket. The temperature will get very, very cold and you will freeze if you stay outside and play."

"How long will I need to sleep?" Gilbert asked.

"All through the long winter," answered Fred. "But there is one day that is kind of fun. You will need to set your clock for it!"

"What day is that?" questioned Gilbert.

"February 2, silly," laughed Fred. "Every year on February 2, groundhogs become a little famous. People wait for the sun to rise and watch to see us peek out of our burrows."

"They do?" replied Gilbert.

"Sure they do," responded Fred. "Listen very carefully. Set your clock for February 2. After you get up, cautiously poke your head out of your hole. If you see something dark and scary, go back into your hole and sleep. There will be six more weeks of bad weather. If you *don't* see anything dark or scary, you can stay awake because bad weather is ending. Spring is just around the corner and everything will be green and fresh once again."

"What does the dark thing look like?" Gilbert asked with a puzzled look on his face.

Fred thought for a long time and then he answered. "It was real big and it wouldn't go away. It followed me around every time I moved. So I jumped right back into my hole and went to sleep. I've been waiting to get another look ever since."

"Bye, Fred!" yelled Gilbert.

"Wait a minute, Gilbert!" Fred hollered. "Where are you going?"

Gilbert stopped running for a moment and called back. "I'm hurrying home before the snow starts to fall. I want to set my clock for February 2 so I don't forget to wake up. I'm not sure I want to see that dark, scary thing, but I *do* want to find out if winter will be gone soon. Thanks for all the information you gave me. I'll see you in February!"

"Good-bye, Gilbert," Fred said smiling. "See you in February."

And they both went home and fell sound asleep.

After You Read

Practice this page with a friend.
One person reads Gilbert's part.
The other person reads Fred's part.
When you are both ready, read it to an adult.

Questions about

Two Groundhog Friends

1. What did people believe would happen if the sun appeared on February 2?

_____

_____

2. When did people begin celebrating Groundhog Day in the United States?

_____

_____

3. Where did Gilbert find Fred? What was Fred doing?

_____

_____

4. What was the reason Fred gave Gilbert for going to sleep?

   ○ He was getting old.   ○ Bears were waking up.

   ○ It was February 2.   ○ Winter was coming.

5. What do you think the dark, scary thing is?

_____

_____

6. How will Gilbert know if spring is on its way?

_____

_____

Tell It in Order

Fred told Gilbert what to do on Groundhog Day. Write the events in the correct order. The first one has been done for you.

First, set the clock for February 2.

Next, _____

_____

Then, _____

_____

Last, _____

_____

What Happened Next?

Number these sentences in order.

_____ He pokes his head out of his hole.

_____ Back into his hole he goes.

_____ The groundhog wakes up on February 2.

_____ Oh, my! He sees his shadow.

_____ There will be six more weeks of winter.

What Does It Mean?

Fill in the circle for the correct answer.

1. What is another word for **groundhog**?

   ○ an opossum   ○ a woodchuck   ○ a cottontail

2. What is another name for **burrow**?

   ○ a den   ○ a mule   ○ a tent

3. What is a **blanket** of snow?

   ○ a quilt made of snowflakes
   ○ fresh snow covering the ground
   ○ a dessert made with snow

4. Find three words in the story that mean the same as **said**.

   _____ _____ _____

5. Read this sentence.

   People wait for the sun to rise and **watch** to see the groundhog.

   What does the word **watch** mean?
   ○ a clock
   ○ a piece of jewelry
   ○ to look

6. Write a sentence using the words **groundhog** and **shadow**.

   _____

   _____

Compound Words

A **compound** word is two words put together to make one new word.

ground + hog = groundhog

A. Find the two smaller words that make each compound word.

1. woodchuck = _____ +_____

2. overnight = _____ +_____

3. snowfall = _____ +_____

4. wintertime = _____ +_____

5. outside = _____ +_____

B. Now make a compound word from each of the two smaller words.

1. spring + time = _____

2. fore + cast = _____

3. sun + shine = _____

4. over + cast = _____

5. sleepy + head = _____

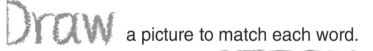 **Draw** a picture to match each word.

ground   hog   groundhog

Silent e

The **e** at the end of a word can make the vowel sound long.
This is called the **silent e**.

tim + e = time   mak + e = make

A. Write the correctly spelled word in each sentence.

1. The sun will _____ at 6:30 in the morning.
   rise   ris

2. A groundhog poked his head out of its _____.
   hol   hole

3. I will _____ you up on February 2.
   wak   wake

4. Gilbert the groundhog knew lots of things about _____.
   life   lif

5. Hurry home! It is _____ for dinner.
   time   tim

6. Fred will _____ from Gilbert inside his burrow.
   hid   hide

7. _____ sure the groundhog doesn't see his shadow.
   Mak   Make

B. Circle the words that have a **silent e** in this poem.

Alone in his burrow and fast asleep,

The woodchuck dreams of springtime, but doesn't make a peep.

He's home in his den all safe and sound,

While above him, the winter snow blankets the ground!

Real or Imaginary?

Talking groundhogs that can predict weather are definitely imaginary. But there are many real facts in the story.

Read the story again and make a list of the real facts you find.

_____

_____

_____

_____

_____

_____

_____

_____

_____

_____

Learn to Be a

Bubbleologist

- Do you like blowing bubbles?
- Are you interested in finding out why bubbles pop?
- Do you want to meet scientists who study bubbles?
- Would you like to find out how long one bubble lasted?
- Are you in third or fourth grade?

If you answered YES to any of these questions, then we have the club for you!

Bubble Blowers Club

The Bubble Blowers Club wants to teach students how to make all kinds of bubbles . . . soap bubbles, gum bubbles, soda bubbles, plastic bubbles, and bubbles you've never heard about! As members you will learn how bubbles have been used to treat some sicknesses like the common flu. You'll also find out how bubbles help make bike helmets stronger.

Join our club and meet other bubble enthusiasts. It's lots of fun!

Sign up at the Children's Museum of Natural History on Thursday at 4:00 P.M. Bring a friend. It's free!

Come pop bubbles with us!

Questions about
Learn to Be a Bubbleologist

1. What does the Bubble Blowers Club want to teach students?

_____

_____

2. Where would you sign up to join the club?

_____

3. Can anybody join the club? Why or why not?

_____

_____

4. What do you think a bubble **enthusiast** is?

_____

_____

5. "Bubble" in the correct answers. If you join the Bubble Blowers Club you will _____ .

○ meet scientists who study bubbles

○ find out why bubbles pop

○ go to New York to see the world's largest bubble

○ find out how long one bubble lasted

○ learn to be a bubbleologist

6. Would you join this club? Why or why not?

_____

_____

Endings and Beginnings

A. The word part **ologist** can be added to the end of a word.
It means "a person who studies in a science or other area of learning."

1. Write **ologist** on the lines to make new words.
   Then draw a line from each word to its meaning.

   zo_____   a person who studies rocks

   bi_____   a person who studies life

   ge_____   a person who studies animals

2. Choose one **ologist** word from above and use it in a sentence.

   _____

   _____

● ▬ ● ▬ ● ▬ ● ▬ ● ▬ ● ▬ ● ▬ ● ▬ ● ▬ ● ▬ ● ▬ ● ▬ ● ▬

B. The word part **sub** can be added to the beginning of a word.
It means "under."

1. Write **sub** on the lines to make new words.
   Then draw a line from each word to its meaning.

   _____marine   below the surface

   _____surface   to place under the water

   _____merge   a ship that can go underwater

2. Choose one **sub** word from above and use it in a sentence.

   _____

   _____

Johnny Appleseed

Johnny Appleseed was born on September 26, 1774. His real name was John Chapman. Life was hard for Johnny as a child. His father had to leave to fight in a war. His mother died when he was still very young.

Johnny's father remarried. He and his new wife had ten children. Johnny spent a lot of time in the nearby apple orchards. He liked the autumn of the year best. That was when the apples were ripe and could be picked. The Chapmans made apple cider, apple butter, and applesauce. Many apples were stored in their cellar for winter. Apples were an important food for Johnny's family. That's why Johnny began saving the apple seeds.

As time went by, Johnny was old enough to leave home. He decided to move west. He carried apple seeds from the family orchards with him. Wherever he went, Johnny would plant apple seeds. He planted his seeds where he thought people might settle.

Johnny became a friend of many of the Indians he met. They taught him many things about the wilderness. They treated him kindly. They liked his friendly smile and gentle ways.

Soon settlers began to move west. Johnny would give families little trees from his orchards. Sometimes people would trade for the trees. Often he would just give them away. Before long, Johnny's apple trees grew everywhere. Folks began to call him Johnny Appleseed. This nickname suited him just fine.

Johnny moved farther west to Ohio. Soon Ohio became too crowded for him. He moved west once again, to Indiana. He cleared more land and planted more trees. No matter where he went, Johnny was welcome. Everyone loved hearing Johnny's stories of his adventures.

Stories about Johnny grew bigger and bigger as time went by. It was told that Johnny slept in the highest trees in a hammock. People said he had a wolf as a pet. Johnny Appleseed became a great hero.

Johnny Appleseed lived to a "ripe" old age. He tended to his apple trees to the very end. He died in Indiana in 1845. But his apple trees and the stories about him kept moving westward. The tale of Johnny Appleseed lives on to this very day!

The Apple Year

Winter

Apple trees are bare and gray. All the leaves have fallen off the branches. The apple trees will rest until spring.

Spring

Apple trees begin growing little knobs that will become the apple blossoms. Pink and white flowers will soon color the branches of the apple tree. Green leaves will remind everyone that warm weather has returned.

Summer

Bees pollinate the apple blossoms. Only now will the tiny green apples begin to grow. Airplanes may fly overhead to spray the trees to protect them from insects. Each day of the summer the apples will grow bigger and bigger.

Autumn

The apples are ready to be picked. Most apples are harvested in late September and early October. The leaves are beginning to fall. Apple trees are getting ready for colder days.

Reading • EMC 4531 • © Evan-Moor Corp.

Questions about

Johnny Appleseed

1. What was Johnny Appleseed's real name?

_____

2. Give two reasons why life was hard for Johnny as a youngster.

_____

_____

3. How did Johnny become interested in apples?

_____

_____

4. Where did Johnny plant his orchards?

_____

_____

5. How did John Chapman become known as Johnny Appleseed?

_____

_____

6. Name the two states in which Johnny planted apple trees.

_____

7. What does this sentence mean to you?

Johnny Appleseed lived to a "ripe" old age.

_____

_____

Tell It in Order

A. Number these events in the order in which they happened in the story.

_____ His travels took him farther west to Ohio.

_____ Johnny was old enough to leave home and move west.

_____ His father had to leave to fight in a war.

_____ He died in Indiana in 1845.

_____ The Indians taught Johnny many things about the wilderness.

_____ John Chapman was born on September 26, 1774.

_____ Fantastic stories about Johnny Appleseed grew.

_____ Soon pioneer families began to arrive.

B. Think about the story of Johnny Appleseed. In the boxes below, draw what you think Johnny would look like at the beginning, middle, and end of the story.

An Apple Tree

Name the parts of the apple tree shown in the picture.

1. _____   4. _____

2. _____   5. _____

3. _____

fruit	bud	flower
pollen	leaves	branch
trunk	knobs	roots

What Does It Mean?

A. Write the number of each word on the line in front of its meaning.

1. orchard	_____ to make a home in a place
2. wilderness	_____ a man admired for his courage, thoughtfulness
3. applesauce	_____ a piece of land where fruit trees grow
4. gentle	_____ to look after; care for
5. settle	_____ an underground room used for storage
6. hero	_____ a region in the wild
7. cellar	_____ soft; kind
8. tend	_____ cooked, mashed apples
9. suited	_____ a hanging bed made of heavy cords
10. hammock	_____ pleased; satisfied

B. Use words from the list above to complete this story summary.

Johnny Appleseed spent much of his time in an apple _____

near his home. He especially liked the fall when the apples were picked.

Many of the apples were stored in the _____.

As time went by, Johnny was old enough to leave home and move west.

He planted apple trees where he thought people might _____.

He traveled across the _____. He became friends with

the Indians and the settlers. He often gave his apple seeds away. Soon

he became known as Johnny Appleseed. People told stories about him and

he became a _____.

The Sounds of A

Read the words. Underline the words that have the **short a** sound.

Circle the words that have the **long a** sound.

Draw an **X** on the words that do <u>not</u> have the long or short sound of **a**.

table	man	after	nature	ax
plant	play	ladder	plain	steak
hard	pause	great	crawl	basket
sauce	name	ask	claim	partner

·········· **Add ed** ··········

A. Change these words by adding **ed**.
Then use each new word in a sentence.

suit_____   tend_____   clear_____

1. _____

2. _____

3. _____

B. Change these words by dropping the **e** before adding **ed**.
Then use each new word in a sentence.

move_____   live_____   settle_____

1. _____

2. _____

3. _____

Alphabetical Order

Write each group of words in alphabetical order.

seeds	1. _____
journey	2. _____
plant	3. _____
trees	4. _____

orchards	1. _____
old	2. _____
Ohio	3. _____
often	4. _____

plant	1. _____
play	2. _____
pick	3. _____
plot	4. _____

 **Draw** two things you can do with an apple.

Spelling ou

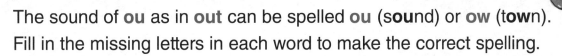

The sound of **ou** as in **out** can be spelled **ou** (**sou**nd) or **ow** (t**ow**n).
Fill in the missing letters in each word to make the correct spelling.

m_____se   h_____se

fr_____n   d_____n

_____t   h_____r

sh_____t   f_____nd

br_____n   h_____

n_____   r_____nd

Pronouns

A **pronoun** is a word that takes the place of a noun.

she	he	I	we	they
him	me	us	them	it

Replace the underlined word or words with a pronoun.

1. <u>Johnny</u> was a great storyteller.   _____

2. The settlers invited <u>Johnny</u> to eat supper.   _____

3. The Indian followed <u>the deer</u>.   _____

4. <u>Johnny and his brothers</u> picked apples in the autumn. _____

5. Ma made a pie with <u>apples</u>.   _____

6. <u>My sister and I</u> like apple pie.   _____

7. The animals liked Johnny. He was a friend to <u>the animals</u>. _____

A Mouse Adventure

It was time to leave the nest. I'd been with my mom and brothers and sisters for the first five weeks of my life. I wanted to explore the outside world. So I packed up a bag. Inside were items that I thought I'd need to have along the way. This included a toothbrush, a change of clothes, extra socks, and, of course, my lucky bottle cap.

My Uncle Louie had found the bottle cap on his travels long ago. He was running from a fierce tabby cat. That's when Uncle Louie discovered it was "lucky." He used it to slide down a grassy hill. The big cat trailed close behind. Thoughts of a delicious "meal on a platter" were on the cat's mind. At the bottom of the hill, Uncle Louie fell into a storm drain. Rushing water began to carry him away. Thinking quickly, he used the bottle cap as a raft. Luckily he was able to guide the raft through the rough waters. He arrived home two days later. He was tired and weak but unharmed. I listened to Uncle Louie tell his incredible story many, many times. One day, to my surprise, he gave me his lucky charm. I have carried it with me ever since.

I thought about Uncle Louie as I carefully put the lucky bottle cap in my pack. Then I gave it a light pat. I was certain that it would come in handy. At some point along the way, I just might need to use it. After that I picked up my knapsack. I headed into the living room where everyone was waiting. My mother was in the doorway holding a small sack. The sack contained a week's worth of meals for me to enjoy.

Each of my brothers and sisters wished me well. Then they gave me some helpful advice.

1. Keep your eyes open for Mr. Owl.
2. Look both ways before crossing a road.
3. Stay away from Mrs. Clark's tabby cat.
4. Never, ever take cheese from a trap!

With that, I said my good-byes. I gave everyone a farewell hug. Then I left the cozy nest that I had known for so long.

Outside the sun was shining. The wooded lot surrounding our mouse hole was alive with activity. Birds were singing from their nests high in the trees. Two squirrels were quarreling over a fat acorn. With each step I took, the excitement of being on my own grew bigger and bigger. Before I knew it, I was scurrying at quite a pace. I found myself far from the safety of my home.

All of a sudden my ears caught the sound of something unusual. I had never heard such a thunderous roar. The sky darkened like night. The wind began to howl. I quickly searched for cover. There was none. The next thing I knew, white stones began pelting the ground. Then it hit me. My bottle cap! I reached into my pack and pulled out my lucky charm. I placed it over my head just as one of the ice balls crashed onto the cap. Stunned, but not hurt, I sat still for some time. Then I smiled. The lucky charm had saved the day and my life!

After You Read

Practice the list of helpful advice. When you can read it quickly with no mistakes, read it to an adult.

As quickly as the storm started, it stopped. The sun returned. A beautiful bow of colors stretched across the sky. I put my bottle cap away. Then I continued on my journey. Before long, day faded into night. The bright yellow moon appeared overhead. A familiar smell pulled me toward a tower in the distance. I kept my nose to the air and followed the scent to the base of the tower. I looked up. Written in big, bold letters were the words *Space Shuttle Mortimer*. I scurried aboard and hid myself in a corner of the huge craft. I sat in the safety of my lucky bottle cap, waiting for the ship to take off.

After a while the countdown began! Ten, nine, eight, seven, six, five, four, three, two, one. Blast off! The shuttle shook fiercely. I held on tightly to my lucky charm with my sharp claws and strong tail. As the ship traveled through space, the pleasant odor grew stronger and stronger. The moon grew bigger through the window of the shuttle. Minutes later, the big ship gently settled on the moon's surface. At that very moment, I realized what the familiar odor was . . . cheese!

Soon the doors opened. Excitedly I crawled out and took a peek. The moon was a huge yellow mound of cheese. Deep craters were filled full of milk. The coldness I felt from being in space quickly turned to warmth. Right away I found a snug hole for shelter. I made a soft nest and fell sound asleep. I made sure my bottle cap was right by my side.

The next morning I woke up early and began nibbling at the moon. What a discovery! The moon really *was* Swiss cheese. What a great adventure this was!

Later in the day I met a moon skunk as well as a milkgator. The three of us became buddies right away. Together we roamed the surface of the moon. We enjoyed fantastic feasts at every stop.

Each day was filled with new discoveries. One day we visited the Apollo landing site. Another day we swam in the milk craters. My favorite day was when I met the man in the moon.

Everything was so exciting at first. Then I began to get homesick. In the distance I heard the roar of the shuttle's engines. I knew it was time for me to head home. I said good-bye to the milkgator. My friend, the moon skunk, walked me back to the ship.

As we were saying good-bye, he handed me a moon crystal. It had been in his family for a long time. He said it was very lucky. Right then I reached into my pack. I took out my bottle cap. It was time to pass my lucky charm on to someone else, too.

Then I loaded my bag of cheese and got aboard the shuttle. I thought of all the stories I would share with my family back home. Then I smiled to myself. The day will surely come when another young mouse is ready for an adventure. He will want to leave the nest and go off on his own. I gave my lucky moon crystal a pat. I'll just keep it with me until then!

Questions about
A Mouse Adventure

1. How did the mouse get the lucky bottle cap?

   ○ He found it on his travels.
   ○ It belonged to his father.
   ○ His uncle gave it to him.

2. Did the mouse's brothers and sisters give him good advice?
   Explain your answer.

   _____

   _____

   _____

3. How did the bottle cap help the mouse the first time?

   ○ It protected him from the falling ice balls.
   ○ It protected him on the space shuttle.
   ○ It helped him make a new friend.

4. What did the little mouse find when he landed on the moon?

   _____

   _____

5. Why did the little mouse give the moon skunk his lucky bottle cap?

   _____

   _____

Draw   what you think a milkgator would look like.

Tell It in Order

Write in order the events that happened to Uncle Louie as he was trying to escape the tabby cat.

First, Uncle Louie used the bottle cap to slide down a grassy hill.

Next, _____

_____

Then, _____

_____

Last, _____

_____

What Happened Next?

Number these sentences in the order in which they happened.

_____The little mouse landed on the moon.

_____ Deep craters were filled with milk.

_____ The little mouse made a soft nest.

_____ The little mouse crawled out and took a peek.

_____ Then the little mouse fell sound asleep.

_____ The little mouse found a snug hole for shelter.

_____ The moon really *was* Swiss cheese.

What Does It Mean?

A. Match each word to its meaning.

knapsack	to argue; find fault
roam	to move around; wander
pelt	a trip
incredible	to hit against
pleasant	a canvas bag carried on the back
quarrel	a suggestion
advice	agreeable
journey	amazing
crystal	a type of rock

B. On the lines below, explain what each phrase means to you.

1. Thoughts of a delicious **meal on a platter** were on the cat's mind.

   _____

   _____

2. A beautiful bow of colors stretched across the sky.

   _____

   _____

Adding Endings

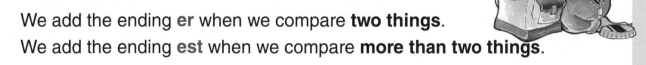

We add the ending **er** when we compare **two things**.
We add the ending **est** when we compare **more than two things**.

Add **er** and **est** to each adjective. Then write a sentence using each word.

small _____ _____

1. _____

    _____

2. _____

    _____

3. _____

    _____

soft _____ _____

1. _____

    _____

2. _____

    _____

3. _____

    _____

Homophones

Words that sound alike but have different spellings and meanings are called **homophones**.

A. Choose the correct homophone to complete each sentence.

herd

heard

1. I _____ my mother calling me.

2. The _____ of cattle will be sold.

cent

scent

1. The candy I bought cost only one _____.

2. The dog followed the _____ to the base of the tree.

nose

knows

1. Uncle Louie _____ the bottle cap is lucky.

2. The little mouse's _____ twitched.

caught

cot

1. We _____ a mouse in the trap.

2. She will sleep on the _____ tonight.

B. **Draw** a picture to show one of the homophones in each pair. Circle the word you drew.

cent   scent   herd   heard   caught   cot

Fact or Opinion?

A **fact** is something that can be proved.
He won the race.

An **opinion** is what someone believes to be true.
No one can run faster than he can.

Make an **X** to show the correct answer.

Fact	Opinion	
_____	_____	The moon is prettier than the sun.
_____	_____	A mouse is a small, furry animal.
_____	_____	The moon is a heavenly body that revolves around the earth.
_____	_____	A mouse has a hairless tail.
_____	_____	A moon skunk is a very friendly animal.
_____	_____	An Apollo spaceship landed on the moon.
_____	_____	Cheese is made with milk.
_____	_____	A mouse is a frightening mammal.
_____	_____	The moon travels around the earth in 29 days, 12 hours, and 44 minutes.
_____	_____	Swiss cheese is delicious.
_____	_____	It would be fun to go to the moon.
_____	_____	A mouse is a rodent.

Why the Leaves Change Color

Did you know that the bright yellow and orange colors we see in leaves in the fall are there all the time, even in the spring and summer? It's true. We just can't see them. How do trees do this magic trick? Read on....

Leaves are a tree's food-maker. There is a special substance in leaves. It is called chlorophyll (klor′ o fil). It is green. The job of chlorophyll is to absorb from sunlight the energy the leaves need to make food for the tree.

In the fall the days become shorter and colder. The leaves stop making food. The chlorophyll breaks down. When this happens we see the yellow and orange colors. The colors were there all along. The green chlorophyll just covered them. Sometimes other substances in the leaves change to turn the leaves red or purple.

Here is a make-believe recipe for a colorful fall.

A Recipe for a Colorful Fall

12 cups of red, yellow, orange, and brown leaves
1 harvest moon
4 cups of frost
3 tablespoons of windy weather
5 teaspoons of chilly nights
1 dash of drizzly rain

Mix together the red, yellow, orange, and brown leaves.
Combine the windy weather with the drizzly rain.
Add the chilly nights.
Then blend in the 4 cups of frost.
Sprinkle everything over the trees in your yard on September 22nd.
Wait for the harvest moon to appear.

Questions about

Why the Leaves Change Color
and
A Recipe for a Colorful Fall

1. Why is chlorophyll important?

   _____

2. Why don't we see yellow or orange leaves in the summer?

   _____

3. Name three colors that leaves may turn in the fall.

   _____

4. Where is the food made in a plant?

   _____

5. Why is there less sunlight in the fall?

   _____

   _____

6. Give two reasons why the recipe is not real.

   _____

   _____

   _____

7. What kinds of ingredients would you use to make a colorful fall?

   _____

   _____

   _____

Fact or Opinion?

A. Write **F** if the statement is a **fact** (something that is true).
Write **O** if the statement is an **opinion** (how someone feels or thinks).

_____ 1. Leaves are very beautiful in the fall.

_____ 2. The days are shorter in the fall.

_____ 3. Chilly nights are good for drinking hot chocolate.

_____ 4. Many leaves turn red, orange, and yellow in the fall.

_____ 5. It is nice to get a little rain in the fall.

_____ 6. Fall is my favorite season.

_____ 7. Leaves make the food for the plant.

_____ 8. Having less sunlight is why leaves start changing colors.

_____ 9. A harvest moon is what makes the fall season so pretty.

_____ 10. Lots of sunlight is needed to keep leaves green.

B. In the box below, draw a picture about fall.

Harriet Tubman

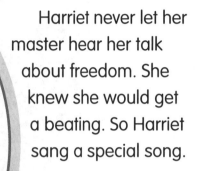

Harriet Tubman was born a slave. The year was 1820. Her family lived in a small village in Maryland. She slept on a straw mattress on the floor of a small house. Every day Harriet awoke before the sun was up. She hurried to her master's house. Her job was to light the fire and then clean the house. She had to do whatever she was told to do. Sometimes Harriet had to work in the fields. She would pick corn all day long. Sometimes she would even pick corn at night. Life was very difficult for Harriet. She and her family and the other slaves worked very hard.

On quiet nights Harriet enjoyed talking to her dad. She liked listening to his stories. Her favorite story was about the children of Israel. Many were slaves just as Harriet was. Moses was their leader. He helped his people get out of Egypt. Maybe she could help her people, too.

Harriet never let her master hear her talk about freedom. She knew she would get a beating. So Harriet sang a special song.

Go down, Moses,
Way down in Egypt's land.
Tell old Pharaoh,
Let my people go!

One night Harriet's family and other slaves began talking. They were talking about places where black people could be free. There were stories about people in the South who did not believe in slavery. Some folks even helped slaves escape to the North. Slavery was not allowed there.

Harriet thought about Moses and the people of Egypt. She began to believe that freedom would someday come to her, too. Then Harriet looked to the sky. She saw the North Star. She knew that the North Star never moved. It was always over the North Pole.

Harriet believed that one day it would guide her north to freedom.

Time passed and Harriet grew older. She also became more determined. She knew that one day she would be free. But right now she needed to be patient.

One afternoon Harriet was working in the fields. She heard other slaves talking. They were talking about something called the Underground Railroad. She learned that the Underground Railroad was not a train *or* underground. It was a road. A road that led to freedom.

A few white folks were helping slaves get to the free states in the North. The slaves were led to freedom along roads and sometimes by water. Safe houses, or stations, were set up. Here they could stop and rest along the way. Harriet promised herself that she would take this road, too.

Soon after this Harriet met a man named John Tubman. John was not owned by a master. He was a free black man. Yet there were many things he could not do. He could not vote. He could not buy land.

Harriet fell in love with John and married him. She was twenty-four years old. John was happy with the way things were. He didn't like Harriet talking about going North. He didn't like Harriet talking about leaving. So Harriet kept her dreams of freedom to herself. One day she would leave the South. She might have to go without her husband.

A few years later Harriet's master died. Harriet did not want to be sold again. She decided that the time had finally come. It was time for her to follow her dreams. Harriet didn't say a word to her husband. She did tell her two brothers, Robert and William. They wanted to go with her. They knew the trip would be very dangerous. It was a chance they wanted to take. She said they would follow the river. It would lead them to the border of Maryland and Delaware. They would travel through forests and swamps. Harriet told them about the North Star. It would always be in front of them as a guide. Her brothers listened to Harriet. She talked about the people who would help them along the way. The Underground Railroad was their ticket out of the South.

The three had not gone very far. Harriet's brothers decided it was too scary. They turned around to go back. Now Harriet was all alone. It was a very frightening time for Harriet. She never gave up. For many nights she traveled through dark forests. The night sounds were very scary. During the day Harriet hid in barns and cellars. Her trip took almost fifteen days. At long last Harriet made it to Pennsylvania. She looked around and made a promise. Harriet promised herself to help other slaves. She would help them use the Underground Railroad just as she had.

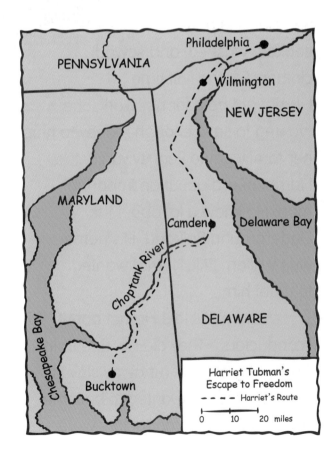

In Pennsylvania, Harriet worked hard. She cleaned houses, cooked, washed, and sewed clothes. For the first time Harriet got paid for her work. She wanted to save enough money to help her family get to Pennsylvania, too. Harriet heard about an important man. He knew a lot about the Underground Railroad. His name was William Still. Harriet wanted to meet him.

William Still told Harriet about "conductors." They did not ride trains. They led groups of runaway slaves to safety. Harriet wanted to become a conductor. The conductors were always men.

Harriet begged Mr. Still to let her try. Finally he agreed.

Harriet made her first trip back to the South. She returned with her sister and two of her sister's children. She brought back many other slaves. Harriet felt so good about helping her people. She made many more trips after this.

All in all, Harriet Tubman helped more than three hundred slaves escape to freedom. She became known as the "Moses of her people." Harriet Tubman was a great woman. She was brave. She followed her dreams. Her dreams also led many others to freedom.

Questions about
Harriet Tubman

1. Why was Harriet always careful not to let her master hear her talking about freedom?

_____

_____

2. How would the North Star help Harriet?

_____

_____

3. What was the Underground Railroad?

   ○ an underground train station
   ○ a train to ride to freedom
   ○ a road to freedom

4. How did the safe houses, or stations, help those on the Underground Railroad?

_____

_____

5. What were **conductors** in this story?

   ○ people who worked on railroads
   ○ people who took slaves to freedom on trains
   ○ people who led runaway slaves to freedom

6. How was Harriet Tubman like Moses of Egypt?

_____

_____

_____

Tell It in Order

A. Number these sentences in the order in which they happened.

_____ Harriet hurried to her master's house.

_____ Sometimes she picked corn into the night.

_____ Harriet awoke before the sun was up.

_____ She lit the fire.

_____ She cleaned house or did whatever she was told.

~~~~~~

B. At long last Harriet made it to Pennsylvania. While in Pennsylvania, Harriet worked hard.

1. What were some of Harriet's first jobs in Pennsylvania?

   _____

2. Harriet got paid for her work. What did she want to do next?

   _____

   _____

3. Last, Harriet met an important man. Who was this man and how did he help Harriet?

   _____

   _____

   _____

What Does It Mean?

Read the words in the box. Think about their meanings in the story of Harriet Tubman. Write each word next to its meaning.

slave	freedom	folks	patient
conductor	stations	master	cellar
underground	Egypt	border	Pharaoh

1. _____ a dividing line between states or countries

2. _____ stopping places along a route or road

3. _____ able to wait for something

4. _____ a person who has power over another

5. _____ a person who guides or leads

6. _____ not being controlled by others

7. _____ a king of old Egypt

8. _____ acting or doing something in secret

9. _____ a person owned by someone else

10. _____ a country in Africa

11. _____ people, or one's family or relatives

12. _____ a room under a building where things are stored

Changing y to i

A. When a verb ends in **y**, we change the **y** to **i** before adding an ending. Change the **y** to **i** and then add the ending given.

1. story (es)   _____

2. study (ed)   _____

3. carry (ed)   _____

4. cry (ed)   _____

5. try (ed)   _____

6. lucky (ly)   _____

7. hungry (ly)   _____

8. happy (ly)   _____

B. Use the words you wrote above to complete these sentences.

1. Harriet loved hearing _____ about the children of Israel.

2. Harriet _____ to help her brothers escape.

3. On many trips, Harriet _____ some of the small children.

4. There were many nights that Harriet _____ for her people.

5. _____, Harriet was able to escape to the North without getting caught.

Contractions

A **contraction** is a shortened form of a pair of words.

A. Write the words that each contraction stands for. Circle the letter or letters that were left out when the contraction was made.

1. it's _____

2. she's _____

3. that's _____

4. he's _____

5. I'll _____

6. we'll _____

7. she'll _____

8. he'll _____

9. wasn't _____

10. isn't _____

11. shouldn't _____

12. couldn't _____

B. Write sentences using four of the contractions above.

1._____

2._____

3._____

4._____

C. Write the contraction for these words.

1. she is _____

2. was not _____

3. we will _____

4. that is _____

Follow the North Star

The story said that the slaves used the North Star to guide them north to freedom. The North Star is easy to find if you first find the Big Dipper constellation. The two stars at the outer edge of the cup point to the North Star.

Use the drawing below. Go outside on a clear night and try to find the North Star.*

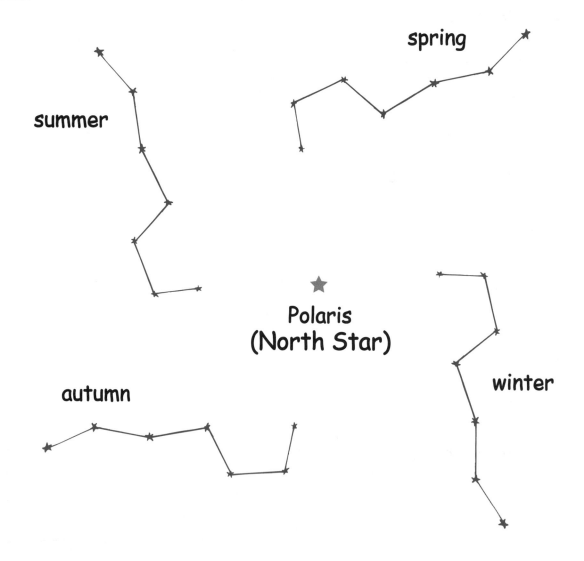

spring

summer

Polaris
(North Star)

autumn

winter

▢ **I found the North Star.**

*You can only do this if you live in the Northern Hemisphere.

The Story of
Little Sparrow

Long ago there lived a young boy. He loved playing outdoors with the animals. He was named Little Sparrow for his black hair. It was as dark as the small bird. One day Little Sparrow went searching for berries. He saw a beautiful, graceful bird soaring across the sky. Quickly Little Sparrow began to follow the bird. The closer he got to the bird, the bigger and stronger the animal seemed. Little Sparrow had never seen a bird such as this. It was strange. Something seemed to be pulling Little Sparrow to the mighty bird.

All of a sudden the bird changed its direction. It swooped down and flew toward Little Sparrow. Little Sparrow was so frightened that he was unable to move. The giant bird grabbed Little Sparrow with his strong claws. It carried him high into the sky.

A large nest was at the top of a great mountain. The bird dropped Little Sparrow softly into its nest. Then it flew away. Little Sparrow was scared. He was all alone and did not know what he should do. He became confused and drowsy. He fell backward into the warm nest. Then he began to dream.

After You Read

Practice your favorite paragraph in this story. Can you use your voice to show how Little Sparrow was feeling? When you are ready, read it to an adult.

In his dream, Little Sparrow felt himself changing into an eagle. He soared high above the clouds. He could see everything for miles around. The earth was green with trees and grasses. Little Sparrow could see animals of every size and shape. He was amazed by the beauty he saw below. He felt a great sense of peace.

Soon the great eagle was flying side by side with Little Sparrow. Together they flew across the great land. They soared over lakes, rivers, and forests. The wonders were endless. Little Sparrow felt peace.

Suddenly feathers began falling from his body. He was not able to fly smoothly. He began to drop from the sky. His fear was so great that he could not cry out. Just as Little Sparrow was about to hit the ground, he awoke from his dream. He was still in the large nest high in the sky. For some strange reason, he was no longer afraid. Little Sparrow stood up and gazed at the beauty all around.

110

As he looked about the nest, he saw large feathers everywhere. He began pulling feathers and straw from the great nest. He used the straw to tie the feathers to his arms and body. He began to feel as powerful as the bird that had carried him away. He leaped from the nest. The wind filled his new wings. It lifted him up and away once again. Little Sparrow began to glide gracefully through the air. Now it was his own strength holding him above the ground below. Never had he known such a magical feeling.

Soon Little Sparrow spotted his home. He flew toward his people. His family and all the members of his village gathered outside their homes. They watched with wonder as Little Sparrow circled above their heads. Then he landed lightly on the ground. Little Sparrow shared the dream and his adventure with everyone. His people knew that he had been given a special gift. A gift from the great bird. From that day on, Little Sparrow was known as Brave Eagle.

In the years that followed, Brave Eagle became chief. He ruled with wisdom and strength. His great-great-grandchildren tell his story today— the story of a boy who learned to face his fears and soar with the great eagle!

Author's note: Stories of brave people and wise animals are told by people all over the world. Some of these stories are true and some are not. *The Story of Little Sparrow* is make-believe, but it is like many Native American tales.

Questions about

The Story of
Little Sparrow

1. Where did the giant bird carry Little Sparrow?

   ○ He carried Little Sparrow to his nest high in the mountains.
   ○ He carried Little Sparrow to his nest by the lake.
   ○ He carried Little Sparrow to his nest in the top of a tall tree.

2. Tell about Little Sparrow's dream.

   _____

   _____

3. How did Little Sparrow escape from the nest?

   ○ He climbed out of the nest and down the mountain.
   ○ He jumped out of the nest and fell to the ground.
   ○ He made wings of feathers and glided away.

4. What gift did the great bird give Little Sparrow?

   _____

   _____

5. Why do you think Little Sparrow became known as Brave Eagle?

   _____

   _____

6. Name two ways you can tell this story is fiction (not true).

   _____

   _____

7. Name two things in the story you think could have really happened.

   _____

Tell It in Order

Draw to show the beginning, middle, and ending of the story. Write about each picture.

What Does It Mean?

Read each sentence below. Use the other words in the sentence to help you figure out the meaning of the underlined word. Fill in the circle for the correct answer.

1. He saw in the distance a beautiful, graceful bird <u>soaring</u> across the sky.
   ○ falling   ○ gliding   ○ leaping

2. The little boy became <u>drowsy</u> as the day turned into night.
   ○ desperate   ○ active   ○ tired

3. He was <u>amazed</u> at the beauty he saw below him.
   ○ pleased   ○ astonished   ○ disappointed

4. The eagle's nest was very high in the air. The boy became lightheaded and <u>confused</u>.
   ○ excited   ○ relaxed   ○ mixed-up

5. Little Sparrow began to feel as <u>powerful</u> as the giant bird.
   ○ beautiful   ○ large   ○ strong

6. The people watched with <u>wonder</u> as Little Sparrow flew above them.
   ○ awe   ○ anger   ○ terror

7. Little Sparrow was <u>gliding</u> high above the ground.
   ○ flapping   ○ moving smoothly ○ spinning

8. When Brave Eagle became chief, he ruled with <u>wisdom</u>.
   ○ no help   ○ many riches   ○ understanding

Listen for the Sound

Read each word. Listen carefully to the sound of the highlighted letter. Write each word in the correct box.

ea**g**le	**c**eiling	brid**ge**	**g**inger	pen**c**il	**c**ereal
a**c**tive	**g**iant	**g**olf	wa**g**on	**g**oldfish	**c**urb
ex**c**ited	**c**andy	**c**elery	**c**atnip	**g**ym	hu**ge**
ma**g**ical	**c**astle	**g**oose	un**c**le	**g**arden	**c**ent

cat /k/

_____

_____

_____

_____

_____

cereal /s/

_____

_____

_____

_____

_____

giant /j/

_____

_____

_____

_____

goat /g/

_____

_____

_____

_____

Base Words and Endings

A **base word** (sometimes called the **starting word** or **root word**) is the main word to which endings can be added.

A. Circle the ending of each word below. Then write the base word on the line. *For example:*

look(ed)   look

1. soaring   _____

2. gathered   _____

3. quickly   _____

4. suddenly   _____

5. leaped   _____

6. searching   _____

7. instantly   _____

8. graceful   _____

9. watched   _____

10. smoothly   _____

B. Now find two more words from the story that have endings. Write them on the lines. Circle the base words.

_____   _____

Many Eagles

There are many kinds of eagles in the world. Use the clues to unscramble the names of the eagles shown below.

___ ___ ___ ___ ___ ___ ___

pensert

eagle

Good thing I'm not afraid of snakes!

___ ___ ___ ___ ___ ___ eagle

gnlode

I must be worth a lot of money.

___ ___ ___ ___ ___ eagle

ckalb

I'm hard to spot in the dark.

___ ___ ___ ___ eagle

hsfi

Perhaps I'll have trout for dinner.

___ ___ ___ ___ eagle

dbla

No, I don't have a wig!

___ ___ ___ eagle

esa

You won't find me in the desert.

BUILDING A PYRAMID

Pyramids are giant tombs. Many years ago the Egyptians buried their kings, or Pharaohs, in these tombs. The first pyramid built was made of stone. It was about 198 feet tall. Workers pulled stone blocks, one at a time, up a long ramp. They then set the blocks into place to make the pyramid shape. The inside of the pyramid had many secret rooms. This is where the king's body was placed. His riches were buried with him.

How to
Make a Pyramid

MATERIALS

2 boxes of sugar cubes
white glue
12" (30.5 cm) square of cardboard
sandpaper

WHAT TO DO

FIRST: The pyramid base is going to be a square. Count out enough sugar cubes to make nine rows of nine. That's 81 cubes. Glue them onto the cardboard.

NEXT: Make the second level by setting glued sugar cubes on top of the base in eight rows of eight.

THEN: Follow the same plan for each level: seven rows of seven, six rows of six, five rows of five, four rows of four, three rows of three, and two rows of two. Put one cube on the top.

LAST: Let your pyramid dry overnight. Sand the sharp corners to make the pyramid smooth.

Questions about
BUILDING A PYRAMID

1. What is a pyramid?

_____

2. Why were pyramids built?

_____

_____

3. How tall was the first pyramid?

_____

4. What materials do you need to build your pyramid?

_____

_____

5. Which of these shows the correct steps to make a pyramid?
   - ○ sand ⟶ glue ⟶ sugar cubes
   - ○ glue ⟶ sugar cubes ⟶ sand
   - ○ sugar cubes ⟶ sand ⟶ glue

6. Which of these sentences tells the main idea of the article?
   - ○ Many Egyptians worked hard.
   - ○ Pyramids were built to bury kings, or Pharaohs.
   - ○ Sugar cubes are sweet.

7. Which of these statements is a fact?
   - ○ Making the pyramids was hard work.
   - ○ The inside of a pyramid had secret rooms.
   - ○ The ancient Egyptians were very smart.

Complete Sentences

> A **complete sentence** tells a complete thought.
> *Example:* The pyramids are very old.
>
> A **fragment** tells only part of a thought.
> *Example:* A king, or Pharaoh.

A. Write a **C** next to each **complete sentence** and an **F** next to each **fragment**.

1. _____ Workers pulled stone blocks up long ramps.

2. _____ The Pharaoh's body.

3. _____ Was made of stone.

4. _____ The inside of a pyramid had many secret rooms.

5. _____ Pyramids are giant tombs.

6. _____ Were put in the tomb.

B. Make each fragment above into a complete sentence.

1._____

2._____

3._____

Silent Letters

Pyramids were **tombs** for the Pharaohs of old Egypt.
In the word **tombs,** the **b** is silent.

A. Cross out the silent letter in each word below.

climb   wrong   know   talks

wrote   listen   knee   sign

B. Write the missing word or words in each sentence.

1. What is _____ with your bicycle?

2. It is important to _____ when your mother

   _____ to you.

3. Do you _____ what that street _____ says?

How Many Syllables?

Write the number of syllables in each word.

1. giant _____   7. secret _____

2. pyramid _____   8. body _____

3. buried _____   9. building _____

4. Egyptians _____   10. sandpaper _____

5. workers _____   11. glue _____

6. riches _____   12. overnight _____

Inuit, the People of the Far North

My name is Kayla. I am Inuit (In' oo it). Inuit are the people who live in the cold Arctic lands. In my language, Inuit means "the people." White people used to call my people Eskimos. We wish to be called Inuit.

I live with my mother, father, and two brothers. We live at the most northern part of the world. It is made up of the Arctic Ocean and the land all around it. For months the sea is covered with thick ice. The land is covered with snow and ice most of the year, too.

Winter is long and very cold. It lasts from October until March. It is dark twenty-four hours a day. The sun does not come up to warm the water and land. When the north winds blow, it is even colder. There are days when the temperature is 50°F (46°C) below zero. My family is prepared. We wear watertight boots. We put on many layers of clothes. Outside we always wear parkas. A parka is a pullover jacket with a hood. The cold winters don't bother me. I guess I'm just used to them.

My family and I look forward to each summer. So much happens in a short time. The temperature stays around 50°F (10°C). A warm day is 60°F (16°C). During the summer the sun shines all day and night. This is why the Arctic is called the "land of the midnight sun."

Summer is my favorite time of the year. The animals and plants come alive. They want to make the most of this short season. I love the sunshine and the beautiful flowers. Some flowers bloom for only a few weeks. Summer doesn't last long, but it is always welcomed.

My people have lived in the Arctic for thousands of years. Long ago they learned to live with the cold weather. These lessons were passed on and on.

My ancestors hunted seals, fish, whales, walrus, and sometimes polar bears. They were very good fishermen and trappers, too. The animals they hunted gave them everything they needed. The meat was used for food. The bones and teeth were made into tools. Fat was melted into oil for heat and light. Animal skins were made into clothing, tents, and boat coverings. Nothing was wasted. Our grandfathers taught us to never take more than is needed.

In the past our people traveled by foot or dog sled. At times boats made traveling easier. A kayak, a one-person boat, was used when an Inuit hunted alone. Bigger hunting groups used a much larger boat called an umiak. Then they could hunt animals like seals, whales, and walruses.

My people lived in huts called innies during the winter. These had whalebone frames covered with moss or sod. Stones were then used to make the outside walls. Inside, the family was warm and safe from the weather.

Some people think the Inuit lived in igloos all year long. That is funny to me. Igloos were made by hunters as they traveled. Igloos were made out of blocks of snow. The blocks were stacked into dome shapes. An igloo could be built in about two hours. The inside of the igloo was heated by burning oil. It was very warm. The hunters could even take off their layers of clothing.

During the summer, tents were used. The women sewed the skins of walruses or seals together. Then they stretched them over a frame of bones. These tents were perfect for summer days. Every Inuit shelter was sturdy and comfortable. They were made to fit each season.

Today, life is very different for me. My family and I live in a modern house. We use electricity for lighting and cooking. We even have a television. Snowmobiles, airplanes, motorboats, and cars help us get around a lot faster. I shop at a nearby store for my clothes. I can also buy CDs and video games. My family buys much of our food there, too. Life is much easier today than it was in the past.

My mom and dad both work at jobs during the day. My brothers and I go to school. We learn math, reading, science, and history. We learn our native language as well as English. School gives us the chance to learn about other cultures. We are learning to use computers and the Internet. These new ideas will help take us into the future.

My brothers and I also learn the old ways of our people. We think that is important. At home we share stories and legends of long ago. On special days we sing the old Inuit songs. We make arts and crafts to decorate our home.

Inuit crafts and carvings are very popular. People in other places want to buy them. Many Inuit people earn a living selling their crafts. It is also a way to share our culture with people around the world.

The Inuit are a very proud people. The Arctic will be our home forever. Our way of life will go on into the future.

Questions about
Inuit, the People of the Far North

1. Who is telling the story?

   _____

2. What does the word **Inuit** mean?

   _____

3. Describe the winter in the Arctic.

   _____

   _____

4. Describe summer weather in the Arctic. How does this compare
   with yours?

   _____

   _____

5. Why is the Arctic known as the "land of the midnight sun"?

   _____

6. Name three ways the Inuit traveled in the old days.

   _____   _____   _____

7. Name three ways the Inuit travel today.

   _____   _____   _____

8. How is Kayla's life like yours? How is it different?

   _____

   _____

   _____

Winter or Summer?

Write a **W** on the line if the sentence tells about **winter** in the Arctic.
Write an **S** on the line if the sentence tells about **summer** in the Arctic.

_____ The Arctic becomes very cold.

_____ It begins around October.

_____ The sun shines all day and night.

_____ Some days it gets to 50 degrees below zero.

_____ Most of the time it's 50 degrees.

_____ This season is short and cool.

_____ When the north winds blow, it's even colder.

_____ Some days it gets to 60 degrees.

_____ Some flowers bloom for only a few weeks.

_____ It lasts until the end of February or March.

_____ We put on many layers of clothing.

_____ The Arctic is called "land of the midnight sun."

What Does It Mean?

A. Fill in the circle for the correct answer.

1. a warm jacket with a hood
   - ○ kayak
   - ○ parka
   - ○ umiak

2. figures or designs cut from
   wood or stone
   - ○ painting
   - ○ drawings
   - ○ carvings

3. the area around the North Pole
   - ○ Antarctic
   - ○ Iceland
   - ○ Arctic

4. a spear used in hunting
   sea animals
   - ○ harpoon
   - ○ lance
   - ○ dagger

5. a one-person boat
   - ○ umiak
   - ○ kayak
   - ○ ferry

6. a large open boat
   - ○ umiak
   - ○ kayak
   - ○ paddle boat

B. Use words from above to complete these sentences.

1. The Inuit used a _____ to hunt whales and seals.

2. At home we share stories and _____ of long ago.

3. Large hunting parties used an _____ to hunt bigger
   animals.

4. On cold winter days we wear a _____.

5. Inuit make _____ of animals to decorate their homes.

6. A _____ was used when an Inuit hunted alone.

7. The _____ is at the northernmost part of the world.

Synonyms

Synonyms are words that have the **same** or **nearly the same** meaning. Choose a word from the box that is a synonym for each underlined word.

shelter	proud	blizzard
boat	clan	jacket
hot	thick	cold

1. The sun was <u>scorching</u> today. _____

2. My family is <u>pleased</u> with my report card. _____

3. The <u>parka</u> will keep me warm. _____

4. The ice on the ocean is very <u>dense</u>. _____

5. An <u>igloo</u> was made by hunters as they traveled. _____

6. The <u>snowstorm</u> lasted two days. _____

7. All the <u>icy</u> weather will be gone by March. _____

8. Our <u>family</u> lives in the cold Arctic. _____

9. A <u>kayak</u> is used on the water. _____

Antonyms

Antonyms are words that have the **opposite** or **nearly the opposite** meaning. Choose a word from the box that is the antonym of each underlined word.

outside	summer	thin
North	night	short
warm	hard	deep

1. The temperature is <u>cool</u> today. _____

2. Do reindeer live in the <u>South</u>? _____

3. My favorite season is <u>winter</u>! _____

4. The water in the pool is <u>shallow</u>. _____

5. The ice on the ocean is very <u>thick</u>. _____

6. I like playing <u>inside</u> with the animals. _____

7. An igloo is <u>easy</u> to build. _____

8. This year the snow lasted a <u>long</u> time. _____

9. Many animals come out during the <u>day</u>. _____

My Favorite Season

Imagine you are an Inuit and live in the far north.

Draw a picture of your favorite season.

Then explain why it is your favorite.

_____

_____

_____

_____

_____

_____

Tracking Form

Topic	Color in each page you complete.					
Juan's Lesson	6	7	8	9	10	11
Shea and the Leprechaun	16	17	18	19	20	21
Owls	26	27	28	29	30	31
A New School Day	33	34				
Animals in Winter	37	38	39	40	41	42
The Proud Turkey	46	47	48	49	50	51
The Seabottom Hotel	53	54				
Bats	58	59	60	61	62	63
Two Groundhog Friends	67	68	69	70	71	72
Learn to Be a Bubbleologist	74	75				
Johnny Appleseed	79	80	81	82	83	84
	85					
A Mouse Adventure	90	91	92	93	94	95
Why the Leaves Change Color	97	98				
Harriet Tubman	103	104	105	106	107	108
The Story of Little Sparrow	112	113	114	115	116	117
Building a Pyramid	120	121	122			
Inuit, the People of the Far North	127	128	129	130	131	132

Answer Key

Checking your child's work is an important part of learning. It allows you to see what your child knows well and what areas need more practice. It also provides an opportunity for you to help your child understand that making mistakes is a part of learning.

When an error is discovered, ask your child to look carefully at the question or problem. Errors often occur through misreading. Your child can quickly correct these errors. Help your child with items she or he finds difficult.

The answer key pages can be used in several ways:

• Remove the answer pages and give the book to your child. Go over the answers as each story and the accompanying activity pages are completed.

• Leave the answer pages in the book and give the practice pages to your child one story unit at a time.

Page 6

Questions about Juan's Lesson

1. What does Juan love more than anything else?
Juan loves playing all sports.

2. Describe Juan's room.
Juan's room is full of sports posters, flags, caps, and equipment. There is a basketball hoop hanging in one corner.

3. What did Juan's mother mean when she said, "Why the long face?"
She wanted to know why Juan looked so sad/upset.

4. Why wasn't Juan happy about the letter?
Juan was told that he would be the backup quarterback and not the first-string quarterback.

5. What lesson did Juan learn from his mother?
Juan learned that each member of a team is very important to the success of the team.

6. What would you have told Juan?
Answers will vary.

Page 7

Tell It in Order

A. Number these events in the order in which they happened in the story.

1 Nobody heard the usual racket coming from Juan's room.
4 Juan showed his mother the letter.
3 He was sitting on his bed, still in his pajamas.
2 Juan's mother hurried up the stairs.
7 Juan decided to be the best backup quarterback.
8 Juan and his dad went out to play football.
6 Juan's mother talked about teamwork.
5 She read the letter aloud.

B. What activities does Juan do before breakfast?
First,
he shoots a few hoops from his bed.

Next,
he runs in place for ten minutes.

Last,
he does twenty-five jumping jacks.

Page 8

What Does It Mean?

A. Choose the correct meaning for each underlined word. Fill in the circle next to the correct answer.

1. Juan has a box for his sports <u>equipment</u>.
○ tools ● supplies ○ hobbies

2. A team <u>depends</u> on all members to do their job.
○ counts ○ wants ● tells

3. The <u>entire</u> crowd clapped and yelled after the touchdown.
○ happy ○ large ● whole

4. You will be a <u>backup</u> quarterback for our team.
○ backward ● standby ○ in front

5. You must learn to play each <u>role</u> you are given.
● part ○ instrument ○ turning

6. He saw all his favorite sports <u>figures</u>.
○ symbols ○ shapes ● people

B. Think about the phrases below. What does each phrase mean to you?

1. It's the ball's in your court.
It's up to you to make the best decision.

2. There's no I in the word **teamwork**.
It takes more than one person to make up a team.

Page 9

Important Ideas

A main idea is an important happening in a story.
A supporting detail is something that tells more about the main idea.

A. Match each main idea from the story to its supporting detail.

Juan loved sports. — You name it. Juan plays it.
Juan spent a lot of time practicing. — Juan's eyes were red. He was still in bed.
Juan was upset about the letter. — Juan's mother and father smiled.
Juan learned an important lesson. — Every morning Juan shoots hoops from bed.
Juan's parents are proud of him. — Every member of a team is important.

B. Find a supporting detail from the story that tells more about the main idea below. Write it on the lines.

Juan's bedroom is full of sports stuff.

He has posters, team flags, and caps on the wall.

Page 10

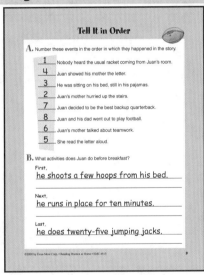

Who Owns It?

We add **'s** to the end of a noun to show that something belongs to it.

A. Write the possessive noun and a word to go with it. The first one has been done for you.

1. Juan — Juan's bedroom
2. mother — **Mother's**
3. father — **Father's**   Answers will vary.
4. brother — **Brother's**
5. sister — **Sister's**
6. coach — **Coach's**

B. Rewrite each phrase using the possessive form of each underlined noun. Remember to add **'s**. The first one has been done for you.

1. the basketball of the <u>boy</u> — the boy's basketball
2. the house of <u>Juan</u> — **Juan's house**
3. the football of the <u>team</u> — **the team's football**
4. the car of the <u>family</u> — **the family's car**
5. the bat of my <u>friend</u> — **my friend's bat**

Page 11

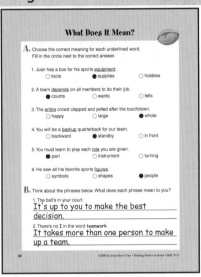

Write It with Feeling!

A sentence that shows strong feeling ends with an **exclamation mark (!)**. Write an exclamatory sentence for each picture. The first one has been done for you.

The player just made a touchdown!

Answers will vary. Possible answers:

Look at that spike!

He's about to be pinned!

She's gathering speed!

Did you remember to begin each sentence with a capital letter and end with an exclamation mark?

Skills: Recalling Story Details; Drawing Conclusions

Questions about
Shea and the Leprechaun

1. What did Shea plan to do on Saint Patrick's Day?
   - ○ go to a Saint Patrick's Day parade
   - ○ go to a leprechaun's party
   - ● go out and catch a leprechaun

2. How did Shea catch the leprechaun?
   - ● She caught the leprechaun in a trap.
   - ○ She grabbed the leprechaun's sleeve.
   - ○ Her dog caught the leprechaun.

3. Why do you suppose the leprechaun didn't run away when Shea let go?
   The leprechaun didn't run away because he knew he could get away whenever he wanted to.

4. How did the leprechaun trick Shea?
   The leprechaun told Shea that his bag of gold would be in the buttercup patch, but it wasn't.

5. What do you think Shea might do next year?
   Shea will not let the leprechaun trick her or let him go.

6. Do you think Shea's mom and dad will believe her when she tells them her story? Why or why not?
   Responses will vary.

16   Reading • EMC 4531 • ©2005 by Evan-Moor Corp.

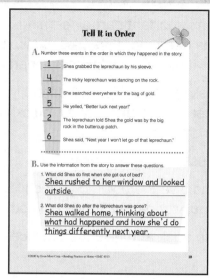

Tell It in Order

A. Number these events in the order in which they happened in the story.

1	Shea grabbed the leprechaun by his sleeve.
4	The tricky leprechaun was dancing on the rock.
3	She searched everywhere for the bag of gold.
5	He yelled, "Better luck next year!"
2	The leprechaun told Shea the gold was by the big rock in the buttercup patch.
6	Shea said, "Next year I won't let go of that leprechaun."

B. Use the information from the story to answer these questions.

1. What did Shea do first when she got out of bed?
   Shea rushed to her window and looked outside.

2. What did Shea do after the leprechaun was gone?
   Shea walked home, thinking about what had happened and how she'd do things differently next year.

©2000 by Evan-Moor Corp. • Reading Practice at Home • EMC 4513   19

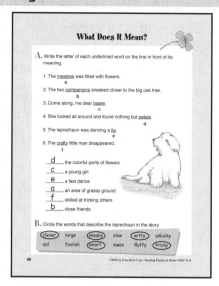

What Does It Mean?

A. Write the letter of each underlined word on the line in front of its meaning.

1. The <u>meadow</u> was filled with flowers. a
2. The two <u>companions</u> sneaked closer to the big oak tree. b
3. Come along, me dear <u>lassie</u>. c
4. She looked all around and found nothing but <u>petals</u>. d
5. The leprechaun was dancing a <u>jig</u>. e
6. The <u>crafty</u> little man disappeared. f

d	the colorful parts of flowers
c	a young girl
e	a fast dance
a	an area of grassy ground
f	skilled at tricking others
b	close friends

B. Circle the words that describe the leprechaun in the story.

(clever) large (sneaky) slow (witty) unlucky
old foolish (smart) mean fluffy (tricky)

20   ©2000 by Evan-Moor Corp. • Reading Practice at Home • EMC 4513

Compound Words

A compound word is two smaller words put together to make one new word. Use the words in the box to make compound words.

butter	rain	every	walk	sun	time
spring	light	cup	bow	where	side

1. buttercup
2. springtime
3. rainbow
4. everywhere
5. sidewalk
6. sunlight

Draw a picture of each compound word below.

buttercup	rainbow
sunlight	butterfly

Drawings will vary.

©2000 by Evan-Moor Corp. • Reading Practice at Home • EMC 4513   21

Words That Describe

Some special words describe things or actions. These words make writing more interesting.

four-leaf	clever	quickly	quietly	yellow
pretty	beautiful	tiny	merrily	

A. Choose the best descriptive word above to complete each sentence.

1. Shea saw a ___tiny___ man dancing by the tree.
2. She picked up the ___four-leaf___ clover.
3. The leprechaun ___quickly___ disappeared.
4. That ___clever___ leprechaun had tricked them again.
5. The ___yellow/pretty___ buttercups smelled sweet.
6. They tiptoed ___quietly___ through the meadow.
7. It was a ___beautiful___ day to catch a leprechaun.
8. The leprechaun laughed ___merrily___ as he held his bag of gold.

B. Write a sentence using two words from the list above.
Sentences will vary.

22   ©2000 by Evan-Moor Corp. • Reading Practice at Home • EMC 4513

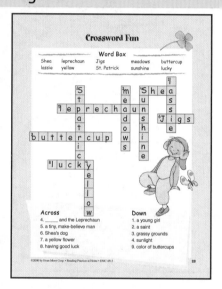

Crossword Fun

Word Box

Shea	leprechaun	Jigs	meadows	buttercup
lassie	yellow	St. Patrick	sunshine	lucky

Across
4. _____ and the Leprechaun
5. a tiny, make-believe man
6. Shea's dog
7. a yellow flower
8. having good luck

Down
1. a young girl
2. a saint
3. grassy grounds
4. sunlight
9. color of buttercups

©2000 by Evan-Moor Corp. • Reading Practice at Home • EMC 4513   23

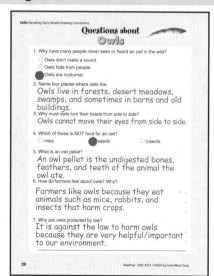

Skills: Recalling Story Details; Drawing Conclusions

Questions about
Owls

1. Why have many people never seen or heard an owl in the wild?
   - ○ Owls don't make a sound.
   - ○ Owls hide from people.
   - ● Owls are nocturnal.

2. Name four places where owls live.
   Owls live in forests, desert meadows, swamps, and sometimes in barns and old buildings.

3. Why must owls turn their heads from side to side?
   Owls cannot move their eyes from side to side.

4. Which of these is NOT food for an owl?
   - ○ mice
   - ● seeds
   - ○ insects

5. What is an owl pellet?
   An owl pellet is the undigested bones, feathers, and teeth of the animal the owl ate.

6. How do farmers feel about owls? Why?
   Farmers like owls because they eat animals such as mice, rabbits, and insects that harm crops.

7. Why are owls protected by law?
   It is against the law to harm owls because they are very helpful/important to our environment.

26   Reading • EMC 4531 • ©2005 by Evan-Moor Corp.

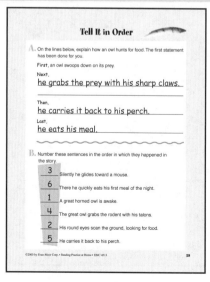

Tell It in Order

A. On the lines below, explain how an owl hunts for food. The first statement has been done for you.

First, an owl swoops down on its prey.

Next, he grabs the prey with his sharp claws.

Then, he carries it back to his perch.

Last, he eats his meal.

B. Number these sentences in the order in which they happened in the story.

3	Silently he glides toward a mouse.
6	There he quickly eats his first meal of the night.
1	A great horned owl is awake.
4	The great owl grabs the rodent with his talons.
2	His round eyes scan the ground, looking for food.
5	He carries it back to his perch.

©2000 by Evan-Moor Corp. • Reading Practice at Home • EMC 4513   29

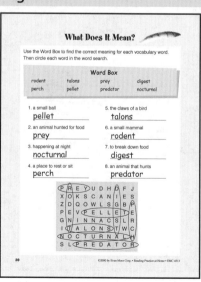

What Does It Mean?

Use the Word Box to find the correct meaning for each vocabulary word. Then circle each word in the word search.

Word Box

rodent	talons	prey	digest
perch	pellet	predator	nocturnal

1. a small ball
   pellet
2. an animal hunted for food
   prey
3. happening at night
   nocturnal
4. a place to rest or sit
   perch
5. the claws of a bird
   talons
6. a small mammal
   rodent
7. to break down food
   digest
8. an animal that hunts
   predator

P	R	E	Y	U	D	H	D	F	J
X	O	K	S	C	A	N	I	E	S
Z	D	Q	O	W	L	S	G	B	P
P	E	V	P	E	L	L	E	T	E
G	N	I	N	N	A	C	S	L	R
I	T	A	L	O	N	S	T	W	C
N	O	C	T	U	R	N	A	L	H
S	L	P	R	E	D	A	T	O	R

30   ©2000 by Evan-Moor Corp. • Reading Practice at Home • EMC 4513

Page 29

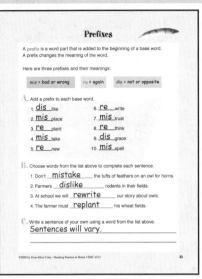

Prefixes

A prefix is a word part that is added to the beginning of a base word.
A prefix changes the meaning of the word.

Here are three prefixes and their meanings:

| mis = bad or wrong | re = again | dis = not or opposite |

A. Add a prefix to each base word.

1. **dis** like
2. **mis** place
3. **re** plant
4. **mis** take
5. **re** new
6. **re** write
7. **mis** trust
8. **re** think
9. **dis** grace
10. **mis** spell

B. Choose words from the list above to complete each sentence.

1. Don't **mistake** the tufts of feathers on an owl for horns.
2. Farmers **dislike** rodents in their fields.
3. At school we will **rewrite** our story about owls.
4. The farmer must **replant** his wheat fields.

C. Write a sentence of your own using a word from the list above.
Sentences will vary.

Page 30

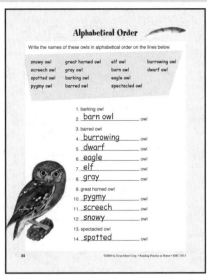

Alphabetical Order

Write the names of these owls in alphabetical order on the lines below.

snowy owl	great horned owl	elf owl	burrowing owl
screech owl	gray owl	barn owl	dwarf owl
spotted owl	barking owl	eagle owl	
pygmy owl	barred owl	spectacled owl	

1. barking owl
2. **barn** owl
3. barred owl
4. **burrowing** owl
5. **dwarf** owl
6. **eagle** owl
7. **elf** owl
8. **gray** owl
9. great horned owl
10. **pygmy** owl
11. **screech** owl
12. **snowy** owl
13. spectacled owl
14. **spotted** owl

Page 31

Whooo's Talking?

Put quotation marks where they belong. The first one has been done for you.

1. The boy yelled, "Look at that beautiful owl!"
2. An elf owl screeched, "I am the smallest owl!"
3. A little girl asked, "Are all owls brown?"
4. The farmer said, "It is nice to have owls eat the mice."
5. A great horned owl screamed, "I am the fiercest of all owls!"

Alike and Different

Elf Owl
- live in giant cactus plants
- smallest owl
- likes warm weather
- lives in southwestern U.S.
- weighs less than one ounce

Both
- are birds
- fly
- have feathers

Great Gray Owl
- largest owl
- weighs 3 pounds
- lives in northern U.S.
- lives in spruce and fir trees

Page 33

Questions about A New School Day

1. Explain why the author says "things start to appear."
When the sun rises, the room becomes light enough for things to be seen.

2. What other sounds from the neighborhood might the author have heard?
Answers will vary.

3. How does the author feel about going to school? How do you know?
The author likes going to school. The author says that he or she is glad to be there and that learning is fun.

4. Do you feel the same way as the author? Explain your answer.
Answers will vary.

Page 34

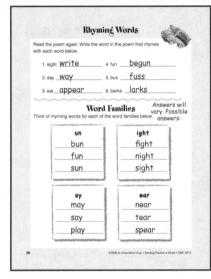

Rhyming Words

Read the poem again. Write the word in the poem that rhymes with each word below.

1. sight **write**
2. day **way**
3. ear **appear**
4. fun **begun**
5. bus **fuss**
6. barks **larks**

Word Families

Think of rhyming words for each of the word families below.
Answers will vary. Possible answers:

un	ight
bun	fight
fun	night
sun	sight

ay	ear
may	near
say	tear
play	spear

Page 37

Questions about Animals in Winter

1. Name the four important ways animals survive during the winter.
Some animals get fat in the fall. Some animals store fresh food. Some animals sleep through the winter. Some animals travel south.

2. How does an extra layer of fat help the moose?
The extra layer of fat is used as energy and warmth.

3. Hibernators are animals that _____.
○ lie in the sun to soak up warmth
● sleep in a dark place all winter
○ travel to a sunny place

4. What do animals that migrate do?
○ sleep all winter
● travel to a warm place
○ spend winter in a cold place

5. Name two things that happen to an animal that hibernates.
The animal's heart beats very slowly and its body temperature drops.

6. What can a heavy coat of hair on animals be compared to?
It is like when we put on our winter coats, mittens, and hats to keep us warm.

Page 38

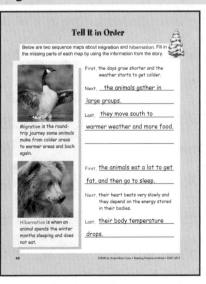

Tell It in Order

Below are two sequence maps about **migration** and **hibernation**. Fill in the missing parts of each map by using the information from the story.

Migration is the round-trip journey some animals make from colder areas to warmer areas and back again.

First, the days grow shorter and the weather starts to get colder.
Next, **the animals gather in large groups.**
Last, **they move south to warmer weather and more food.**

Hibernation is when an animal spends the winter months sleeping and does not eat.

First, **the animals eat a lot to get fat, and then go to sleep.**
Next, their heart beats very slowly and they depend on the energy stored in their bodies.
Last, **their body temperature drops.**

Page 39

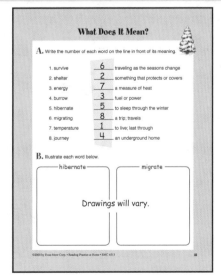

What Does It Mean?

A. Write the number of each word on the line in front of its meaning.

1. survive
2. shelter
3. energy
4. burrow
5. hibernate
6. migrating
7. temperature
8. journey

6 traveling as the seasons change
2 something that protects or covers
7 a measure of heat
3 fuel or power
5 to sleep through the winter
8 a trip; travels
1 to live; last through
4 an underground home

B. Illustrate each word below.

| hibernate | migrate |

Drawings will vary.

Page 40

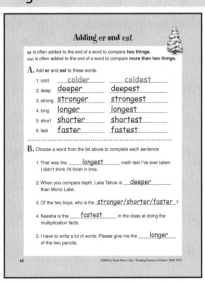

Adding er and est

er is often added to the end of a word to compare **two things**.
est is often added to the end of a word to compare **more than two things**.

A. Add **er** and **est** to these words.

1. cold — **colder** — **coldest**
2. deep — **deeper** — **deepest**
3. strong — **stronger** — **strongest**
4. long — **longer** — **longest**
5. short — **shorter** — **shortest**
6. fast — **faster** — **fastest**

B. Choose a word from the list above to complete each sentence.

1. That was the **longest** math test I've ever taken. I didn't think I'd finish in time.
2. When you compare depth, Lake Tahoe is **deeper** than Mono Lake.
3. Of the two boys, who is the **stronger/shorter/faster**?
4. Keesha is the **fastest** in the class at doing the multiplication facts.
5. I have to write a lot of words. Please give me the **longer** of the two pencils.

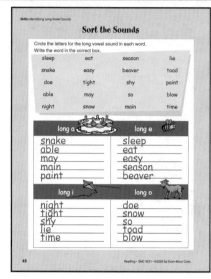

Change y to i

A. Change the y to an i and then add the ending given for each word.

1. body (es)   **bodies**
2. try (es)   **tries**
3. busy (ly)   **busily**
4. empty (ed)   **emptied**
5. bury (ed)   **buried**
6. easy (ly)   **easily**

B. Choose a word from the list above to complete each sentence.

1. The squirrel **buried** the acorn to save it for winter.
2. A hungry elk **tried** to find food under the deep snow.
3. All of the strongest animals **easily** survived the winter.
4. The chipmunk is **busily** putting food for the winter in its burrow.
5. Hibernators use the energy stored in their **bodies** to keep them alive through the cold months.

Skill: Identifying Long Vowel Sounds

Sort the Sounds

Circle the letters for the long vowel sound in each word. Write the word in the correct box.

sleep	eat	season	lie
snake	easy	beaver	toad
doe	tight	shy	paint
able	may	so	blow
night	snow	main	time

long a
snake
able
may
main
paint

long e
sleep
eat
easy
season
beaver

long i
night
tight
shy
lie
time

long o
doe
snow
so
toad
blow

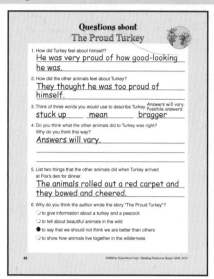

Questions about The Proud Turkey

1. How did Turkey feel about himself?
He was very proud of how good-looking he was.

2. How did the other animals feel about Turkey?
They thought he was too proud of himself.

3. Think of three words you would use to describe Turkey. *Answers will vary. Possible answers:*
stuck up   **mean**   **bragger**

4. Do you think what the other animals did to Turkey was right? Why do you think this way?
Answers will vary.

5. List two things that the other animals did when Turkey arrived at Fox's den for dinner.
The animals rolled out a red carpet and they bowed and cheered.

6. Why do you think the author wrote the story "The Proud Turkey"?
○ to give information about a turkey and a peacock
○ to tell about beautiful animals in the wild
● to say that we should not think we are better than others
○ to show how animals live together in the wilderness

Tell It in Order

Number these events in the order in which they happened in the story.

6 The turkey choked on a tart.
4 All the animals invited the turkey to dinner.
5 A peacock entered the dining room.
8 The animals asked the wise owl for help.
1 Every day the turkey would brag about himself.
3 The porcupine scribbled an invitation to the turkey.
10 All the animals planned another party with no surprises.
9 The turkey was roosting in an old oak tree.
7 The only sound the turkey could make was, "Gobble, gobble, gobble."
2 The animals thought the turkey was too proud.

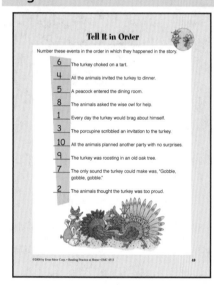

What Does It Mean?

Word Box
preen   rude   roost   humble   horrified   approached
clever   brag   mirror   carpet   tart   waddled

(crossword puzzle with answers: clever, mirror, waddled, horrified, approached, humble, roost, preen, brag, tart)

Across
1. showing a quick mind; smart
3. a surface that reflects light
4. moved from side to side when walking
6. shocked; filled with alarm
9. a small pie
10. to clean or trim with the beak

Down
1. rug; fabric floor covering
2. impolite
5. came near to
6. not speaking too highly of oneself
7. a resting place where birds perch
8. to speak with too much pride about oneself

Add an Ending

A. Add endings to these words.

	er	est
1. kind	kinder	kindest
2. proud	prouder	proudest
3. grand	grander	grandest
4. quick	quicker	quickest
5. quiet	quieter	quietest

B. Use the words above to complete these sentences.

1. A fox can run **quicker** than a porcupine.
2. Standing in the middle of a forest is one of the **quietest** places I know.
3. Saving an owl from dying is one of the things I am **proudest** of.
4. At the beginning of the story, all the other animals were **kinder** than the turkey.
5. At the end of the story, the fox made an even **grander** dinner for the turkey.

Word Pyramids

A. Think about the story "The Proud Turkey." Use words from the story to help you create a word pyramid about the turkey.

Follow these directions:
Line 1: Topic (This one has been done for you.)
Line 2: Two words describing the topic
Line 3: Three words that show his actions
Line 4: Four words describing his feelings

Answers will vary. Possible answers:

Turkey
proud   beautiful
brag   show off   boast
excited   shocked   horrified   sad

B. Make your own word pyramid about an animal of your choice.

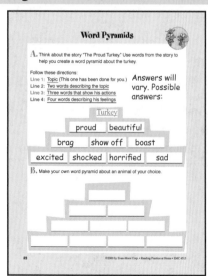

Making Comparisons

For each statement, make an X in the correct box.

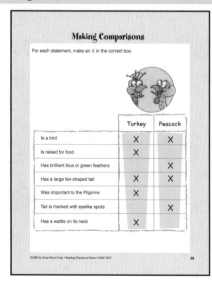

	Turkey	Peacock
Is a bird	X	X
Is raised for food	X	
Has brilliant blue or green feathers		X
Has a large fan-shaped tail	X	X
Was important to the Pilgrims	X	
Tail is marked with eyelike spots		X
Has a wattle on its neck	X	

Skill: Recalling Story Details; Drawing Conclusions; Expressing an Opinion

Questions about The Seabottom Hotel

1. Why do you think the hotel is named the Seabottom Hotel?
The hotel is on the bottom of the Blue Sea.

2. What can be seen from every window?
● rare undersea animals
○ tall buildings
○ strange and unusual trees

3. What do you get to do with the tuna?
○ eat the tuna
○ catch the tuna
● swim with the tuna

4. Why do you think no one is ever "crabby" at the hotel?
Answers will vary.

5. Why is sunscreen not needed when you visit the Seabottom Hotel?
Sunscreen is not needed because the hotel is underwater.

6. How will you get to the hotel?
○ by airplane
○ by ocean liner
● by submarine

7. Would you like to vacation at the Seabottom Hotel? Tell why or why not.
Answers will vary.

Page 54

Nouns

A noun is a word that names a **person, place,** or **thing.**

A. Write each noun under the correct heading.

sea star	diver	hotel
seabottom	seahorse	golfer
shell	singer	inn
swordfish	waiter	airport
child	golf course	octopus

Person	Place	Thing
child	seabottom	sea star
diver	golf course	shell
singer	hotel	swordfish
waiter	inn	seahorse
golfer	airport	octopus

B. Choose one noun from each of the headings above. Then write three sentences using those nouns.

1. _____ Sentences will vary. _____
2. _____
3. _____

Page 58

Questions about Bats

1. Name two things people once thought about bats that are not true.
People thought bats were birds.
People thought bats were blind.

2. Name three places where you could look to find a bat.
Bats can be found in caves, hollow trees,
attics, and old buildings.

3. Give two reasons why bats are mammals.
Bats are mammals because they are
warm-blooded and they feed their
babies milk.

4. Why has the number of bats declined over the past years?
Some bats' habitats are being
destroyed, and some bats are being
hunted and trapped.

5. Do you think it is important to save bats? Why or why not?
_____ Answers will vary. _____

6. Give two facts about bats that you thought were the most interesting.
_____ Answers will vary. _____

Page 59

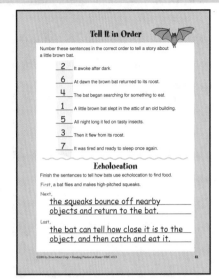

Tell It in Order

Number these sentences in the correct order to tell a story about a little brown bat.

- 2 It awoke after dark.
- 6 At dawn the brown bat returned to its roost.
- 4 The bat began searching for something to eat.
- 1 A little brown bat slept in the attic of an old building.
- 5 All night long it fed on tasty insects.
- 3 Then it flew from its roost.
- 7 It was tired and ready to sleep once again.

Echolocation

Finish the sentences to tell how bats use echolocation to find food.

First, a bat flies and makes high-pitched squeaks.

Next,
the squeaks bounce off nearby
objects and return to the bat.

Last,
the bat can tell how close it is to the
object, and then catch and eat it.

Page 60

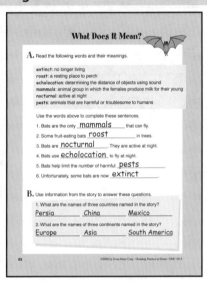

What Does It Mean?

A. Read the following words and their meanings.

extinct: no longer living
roost: a resting place to perch
echolocation: determining the distance of objects using sound
mammals: animal group in which the females produce milk for their young
nocturnal: active at night
pests: animals that are harmful or troublesome to humans

Use the words above to complete these sentences.

1. Bats are the only _mammals_ that can fly.
2. Some fruit-eating bats _roost_ in trees.
3. Bats are _nocturnal_. They are active at night.
4. Bats use _echolocation_ to fly at night.
5. Bats help limit the number of harmful _pests_.
6. Unfortunately, some bats are now _extinct_.

B. Use information from the story to answer these questions.

1. What are the names of three countries named in the story?
Persia _China_ _Mexico_

2. What are the names of three continents named in the story?
Europe _Asia_ _South America_

Page 61

More Than One

Most nouns are made plural by just adding s.
Nouns that end in s, ch, sh, or x are made plural by adding es.

A. Write the plural of each of these nouns by adding s or es.

1. bat _bats_
2. fruit _fruits_
3. animal _animals_
4. human _humans_
5. bird _birds_
6. flying fox _flying foxes_
7. cave _caves_
8. frog _frogs_
9. tree _trees_
10. moth _moths_
11. mammal _mammals_
12. female _females_

B. Choose three of the new words you made above. Use each word in a question about bats. Remember to use a question mark (?).

Example: Did you know that bats are the only mammals that fly?

1. _____ Questions will vary. _____
2. _____
3. _____

Page 62

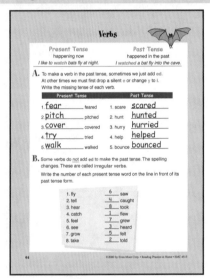

Verbs

Present Tense	Past Tense
happening now	happened in the past
I like to *watch* bats fly at night.	I *watched* a bat fly into the cave.

A. To make a verb in the past tense, sometimes we just add ed.
At other times we must first drop a silent e or change y to i.
Write the missing tense of each verb.

Present Tense		Past Tense	
1. fear	feared	1. scare	scared
2. pitch	pitched	2. hunt	hunted
3. cover	covered	3. hurry	hurried
4. try	tried	4. help	helped
5. walk	walked	5. bounce	bounced

B. Some verbs do not add ed to make the past tense. The spelling changes. These are called irregular verbs.

Write the number of each present tense word on the line in front of its past tense form.

1. fly	6 saw
2. tell	4 caught
3. hear	8 took
4. catch	1 flew
5. feel	7 grew
6. see	3 heard
7. grow	5 felt
8. take	2 told

Page 63

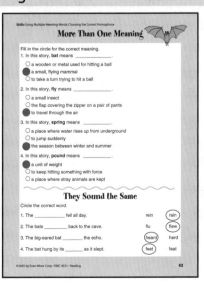

Skills: Using Multiple-Meaning Words/Choosing the Correct Homophone

More Than One Meaning

Fill in the circle for the correct meaning.

1. In this story, **bat** means _____.
- ○ a wooden or metal used for hitting a ball
- ● a small, flying mammal
- ○ to take a turn trying to hit a ball

2. In this story, **fly** means _____.
- ○ a small insect
- ○ the flap covering the zipper on a pair of pants
- ● to travel through the air

3. In this story, **spring** means _____.
- ○ a place where water rises up from underground
- ○ to jump suddenly
- ● the season between winter and summer

4. In this story, **pound** means _____.
- ● a unit of weight
- ○ to keep hitting something with force
- ○ a place where stray animals are kept

They Sound the Same

Circle the correct word.

1. The _____ fell all day. rein (rain)
2. The bats _____ back to the cave. flu (flew)
3. The big-eared bat _____ the echo. (heard) herd
4. The bat hung by its _____ as it slept. (feet) feat

Page 67

Questions about Two Groundhog Friends

1. What did people believe would happen if the sun appeared on February 2?
If the sun appeared and the groundhog
saw its shadow, people believed there
would be six more weeks of summer.

2. When did people begin celebrating Groundhog Day in the United States?
People began celebrating Groundhog
Day in the early 1880s.

3. Where did Gilbert find Fred? What was Fred doing?
Gilbert found Fred near his burrow,
lying in the warm sun.

4. What was the reason Fred gave Gilbert for going to sleep?
- ○ He was getting old.   ○ Bears were waking up.
- ○ It was February 2.   ● Winter was coming.

5. What do you think the dark, scary thing is?
The dark, scary thing would be the
groundhog's shadow.

6. How will Gilbert know if spring is on its way?
If Gilbert doesn't see his shadow, then
he'll know spring is on its way.

Page 68

Tell It in Order

Fred told Gilbert what to do on Groundhog Day. Write the events in the correct order. The first one has been done for you.

First, set the clock for February 2.

Next, get up.

Then, poke your head out your hole.

Last, if you see something dark and
scary, go back to sleep. If you don't,
you can stay awake.

What Happened Next?

Number these sentences in order.

- 2 He pokes his head out of his hole.
- 4 Back into his hole he goes.
- 1 The groundhog wakes up on February 2.
- 3 Oh, my! He sees his shadow.
- 5 There will be six more weeks of winter.

Page 69

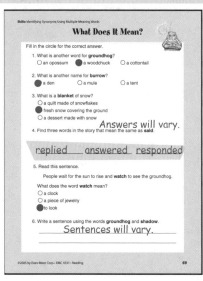

Skills: Identifying Synonyms; Using Multiple-Meaning Words

What Does It Mean?

Fill in the circle for the correct answer.

1. What is another word for **groundhog**?
   ○ an opossum ● a woodchuck ○ a cottontail

2. What is another name for **burrow**?
   ● a den ○ a mule ○ a tent

3. What is a **blanket** of snow?
   ○ a quilt made of snowflakes
   ● fresh snow covering the ground
   ○ a dessert made with snow

4. Find three words in the story that mean the same as **said**.

   Answers will vary.

   replied   answered   responded

5. Read this sentence.

   People wait for the sun to rise and **watch** to see the groundhog.

   What does the word **watch** mean?
   ○ a clock
   ○ a piece of jewelry
   ● to look

6. Write a sentence using the words **groundhog** and **shadow**.
   Sentences will vary.

©2005 by Evan-Moor Corp. • EMC 4531 • Reading   69

Page 70

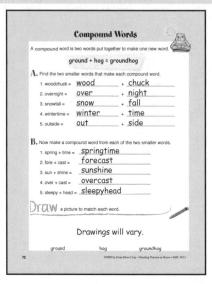

Compound Words

A compound word is two words put together to make one new word.

ground + hog = groundhog

A. Find the two smaller words that make each compound word.

1. woodchuck = __wood__ + __chuck__
2. overnight = __over__ + __night__
3. snowfall = __snow__ + __fall__
4. wintertime = __winter__ + __time__
5. outside = __out__ + __side__

B. Now make a compound word from each of the two smaller words.

1. spring + time = __springtime__
2. fore + cast = __forecast__
3. sun + shine = __sunshine__
4. over + cast = __overcast__
5. sleepy + head = __sleepyhead__

Draw a picture to match each word.

Drawings will vary.

ground   hog   groundhog

©2000 by Evan-Moor Corp. • Reading Practice at Home • EMC 4513   72

Page 71

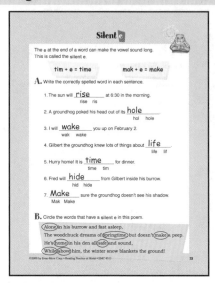

Silent e

The e at the end of a word can make the vowel sound long. This is called the silent e.

tim + e = time   mak + e = make

A. Write the correctly spelled word in each sentence.

1. The sun will __rise__ at 6:30 in the morning.
   rise ris

2. A groundhog poked his head out of its __hole__
   hol hole

3. I will __wake__ you up on February 2.
   wak wake

4. Gilbert the groundhog knew lots of things about __life__
   life lif

5. Hurry home! It is __time__ for dinner.
   time tim

6. Fred will __hide__ from Gilbert inside his burrow.
   hid hide

7. __Make__ sure the groundhog doesn't see his shadow.
   Mak Make

B. Circle the words that have a silent e in this poem.

(Alone) in his burrow and fast asleep,
The woodchuck dreams of (springtime) but doesn't (make) a peep.
He's (home) in his den all (safe) and sound,
(While) (above) him, the winter snow blankets the ground!

©2000 by Evan-Moor Corp. • Reading Practice at Home • EMC 4513   73

Page 72

Skills: Distinguishing Real Events from Imaginary Events; Creating a List

Real or Imaginary?

Talking groundhogs that can predict weather are definitely imaginary. But there are many real facts in the story.

Read the story again and make a list of the real facts you find.

also called woodchucks
live in burrows
sleep in winter
live near fields and meadows
like to bask in the sun
come out of burrows early in morning

72   Reading • EMC 4531 • ©2005 by Evan-Moor Corp.

Page 74

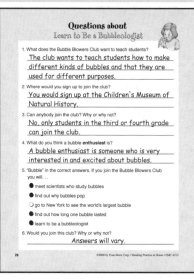

Questions about
Learn to Be a Bubbleologist

1. What does the Bubble Blowers Club want to teach students?
   The club wants to teach students how to make different kinds of bubbles and that they are used for different purposes.

2. Where would you sign up to join the club?
   You would sign up at the Children's Museum of Natural History.

3. Can anybody join the club? Why or why not?
   No, only students in the third or fourth grade can join the club.

4. What do you think a bubble **enthusiast** is?
   A bubble enthusiast is someone who is very interested in and excited about bubbles.

5. "Bubble" in the correct answers. If you join the Bubble Blowers Club you will. . .
   ● meet scientists who study bubbles
   ● find out why bubbles pop
   ○ go to New York to see the world's largest bubble
   ● find out how long one bubble lasted
   ● learn to be a bubbleologist

6. Would you join this club? Why or why not?
   Answers will vary.

©2000 by Evan-Moor Corp. • Reading Practice at Home • EMC 4513   76

Page 75

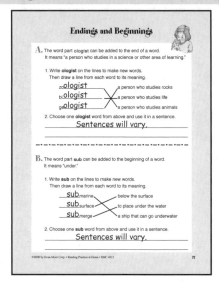

Endings and Beginnings

A. The word part ologist can be added to the end of a word. It means "a person who studies in a science or other area of learning."

1. Write **ologist** on the lines to make new words. Then draw a line from each word to its meaning.
   zo__ologist__   a person who studies rocks
   b__ologist__   a person who studies life
   g__ologist__   a person who studies animals

2. Choose one **ologist** word from above and use it in a sentence.
   Sentences will vary.

B. The word part **sub** can be added to the beginning of a word. It means "under."

1. Write **sub** on the lines to make new words. Then draw a line from each word to its meaning.
   __sub__marine   below the surface
   __sub__surface   to place under the water
   __sub__merge   a ship that can go underwater

2. Choose one **sub** word from above and use it in a sentence.
   Sentences will vary.

©2000 by Evan-Moor Corp. • Reading Practice at Home • EMC 4513   77

Page 79

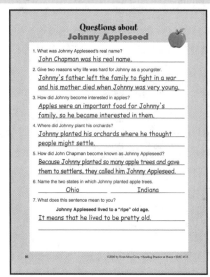

Questions about
Johnny Appleseed

1. What was Johnny Appleseed's real name?
   John Chapman was his real name.

2. Give two reasons why life was hard for Johnny as a youngster.
   Johnny's father left the family to fight in a war and his mother died when Johnny was very young.

3. How did Johnny become interested in apples?
   Apples were an important food for Johnny's family, so he became interested in them.

4. Where did Johnny plant his orchards?
   Johnny planted his orchards where he thought people might settle.

5. How did John Chapman become known as Johnny Appleseed?
   Because Johnny planted so many apple trees and gave them to settlers, they called him Johnny Appleseed.

6. Name the two states in which Johnny planted apple trees.
   Ohio   Indiana

7. What does this sentence mean to you?
   Johnny Appleseed lived to a "ripe" old age.
   It means that he lived to be pretty old.

81   ©2000 by Evan-Moor Corp. • Reading Practice at Home • EMC 4513

Page 80

Tell It in Order

A. Number these events in the order in which they happened in the story.

   __6__ His travels took him farther west to Ohio.
   __3__ Johnny was old enough to leave home and move west.
   __2__ His father had to leave to fight in a war.
   __8__ He died in Indiana in 1845.
   __4__ The Indians taught Johnny many things about the wilderness.
   __1__ John Chapman was born on September 26, 1774.
   __7__ Fantastic stories about Johnny Appleseed grew.
   __5__ Soon pioneer families began to arrive.

B. Think about the story of Johnny Appleseed. In the boxes below, draw what you think Johnny would look like at the beginning, middle, and end of the story.

Drawings will vary.

©2000 by Evan-Moor Corp. • Reading Practice at Home • EMC 4513   82

Page 81

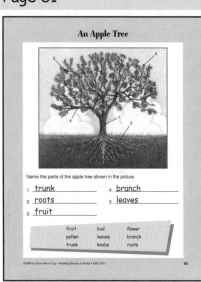

An Apple Tree

Name the parts of the apple tree shown in the picture.

1. __trunk__   4. __branch__
2. __roots__   5. __leaves__
3. __fruit__

fruit	bud	flower
pollen	leaves	branch
trunk	knobs	roots

©2000 by Evan-Moor Corp. • Reading Practice at Home • EMC 4513   83

Page 82 — What Does It Mean?

A. Write the number of each word on the line in front of its meaning.

1. orchard — **5** to make a home in a place
2. wilderness — **6** a man admired for his courage, thoughtfulness
3. applesauce — **1** a piece of land where fruit trees grow
4. gentle — **8** to look after; care for
5. settle — **7** an underground room used for storage
6. hero — **2** a region in the wild
7. cellar — **4** soft; kind
8. tend — **3** cooked, mashed apples
9. suited — **10** a hanging bed made of heavy cords
10. hammock — **9** pleased; satisfied

B. Use words from the list above to complete this story summary.

Johnny Appleseed spent much of his time in an apple **orchard** near his home. He especially liked the fall when the apples were picked. Many of the apples were stored in the **cellar**

As time went by, Johnny was old enough to leave home and move west. He planted apple trees where he thought people might **settle** He traveled across the **wilderness** He became friends with the Indians and the settlers. He often gave his apple seeds away. Soon he became known as Johnny Appleseed. People told stories about him and he became a **hero**

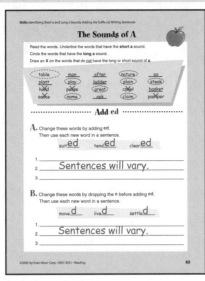

Page 83 — The Sounds of A

Read the words. Underline the words that have the **short a** sound. Circle the words that have the **long a** sound. Draw an **X** on the words that do not have the long or short sound of **a**.

(table) — man — after — (nature) — ax
plant — (play) — ladder — (plain) — steak
hand — pause — great — crawl — (claim)
sauce — (name) — ask — (claim) — partner

—————— Add ed ——————

A. Change these words by adding ed. Then use each new word in a sentence.
suit**ed**   tend**ed**   clear**ed**

1.
2. Sentences will vary.
3.

B. Change these words by dropping the e before adding ed. Then use each new word in a sentence.
move**d**   live**d**   settle**d**

1.
2. Sentences will vary.
3.

Page 84 — Alphabetical Order

Write each group of words in alphabetical order.

seeds	1. **journey**
journey	2. **plant**
plant	3. **seeds**
trees	4. **trees**

orchards	1. **often**
old	2. **Ohio**
Ohio	3. **old**
often	4. **orchards**

plant	1. **pick**
play	2. **plant**
pick	3. **play**
plot	4. **plot**

Draw two things you can do with an apple.

Drawings will vary.

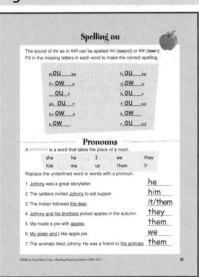

Page 85 — Spelling ou

The sound of ou as in out can be spelled ou (sound) or ow (town). Fill in the missing letters in each word to make the correct spelling.

m**ou**se   h**ou**se
fr**ow**n   d**ow**n
out   h**ou**r
sh**ou**t   f**ou**nd
br**ow**n   h**ow**l
n**ow**   r**ou**nd

Pronouns

A pronoun is a word that takes the place of a noun.

she   he   I   we   they
him   me   us   them   it

Replace the underlined word or words with a pronoun.

1. Johnny was a great storyteller. — **he**
2. The settlers invited Johnny to eat supper. — **him**
3. The Indian followed the deer. — **it/them**
4. Johnny and his brothers picked apples in the autumn. — **they**
5. Ma made a pie with apples. — **them**
6. My sister and I like apple pie. — **we**
7. The animals liked Johnny. He was a friend to the animals. — **them**

Page 90 — Questions about A Mouse Adventure

1. How did the mouse get the lucky bottle cap?
○ He found it on his travels.
○ It belonged to his father.
● His uncle gave it to him.

2. Did the mouse's brothers and sisters give him good advice? Explain your answer.
Yes, they gave him good advice. They told him things that would keep him safe.

3. How did the bottle cap help the mouse the first time?
● It protected him from the falling ice balls.
○ It protected him on the space shuttle.
○ It helped him make a new friend.

4. What did the little mouse find when he landed on the moon?
The mouse found out that the moon was made of swiss cheese and that the craters were full of milk.

5. Why did the little mouse give the moon skunk his lucky bottle cap?
The mouse gave his bottle cap to the moon skunk because the skunk gave him his moon crystal.

Draw what you think a milkgator would look like.
Drawings will vary.

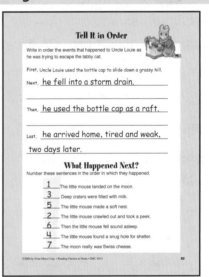

Page 91 — Tell It in Order

Write in order the events that happened to Uncle Louie as he was trying to escape the tabby cat.

First, Uncle Louie used the bottle cap to slide down a grassy hill.

Next, **he fell into a storm drain.**

Then, **he used the bottle cap as a raft.**

Last, **he arrived home, tired and weak, two days later.**

What Happened Next?

Number these sentences in the order in which they happened.

1 The little mouse landed on the moon.
3 Deep craters were filled with milk.
5 The little mouse made a soft nest.
2 The little mouse crawled out and took a peek.
6 Then the little mouse fell sound asleep.
4 The little mouse found a snug hole for shelter.
7 The moon really was Swiss cheese.

Page 92 — What Does It Mean?

A. Match each word to its meaning.

knapsack — to argue; find fault
roam — to move around; wander
pelt — a trip
incredible — to hit against
pleasant — a canvas bag carried on the back
quarrel — a suggestion
advice — agreeable
journey — amazing
crystal — a type of rock

B. On the lines below, explain what each phrase means to you.
Answers will vary. Possible answers:

1. Thoughts of a delicious **meal on a platter** were on the cat's mind.
a mouse served on a plate for dinner

2. A beautiful **bow of colors** stretched across the sky.
a rainbow

Page 93 — Adding Endings

We add the ending er when we compare **two things**.
We add the ending est when we compare **more than two things**.

Add er and est to each adjective. Then write a sentence using each word.

small — **smaller** — **smallest**
1.
2. Sentences will vary.
3.

soft — **softer** — **softest**
1.
2. Sentences will vary.
3.

Page 94 — Homophones

Words that sound alike but have different spellings and meanings are called homophones.

A. Choose the correct homophone to complete each sentence.

herd / heard
1. I **heard** my mother calling me.
2. The **herd** of cattle will be sold.

cent / scent
1. The candy I bought cost only one **cent**
2. The dog followed the **scent** to the base of the tree.

nose / knows
1. Uncle Louie **knows** the bottle cap is lucky.
2. The little mouse's **nose** twitched.

caught / cot
1. We **caught** a mouse in the trap.
2. She will sleep on the **cot** tonight.

B. Draw a picture to show one of the homophones in each pair. Circle the word you drew.

Drawings will vary.

cent scent   herd heard   caught cot

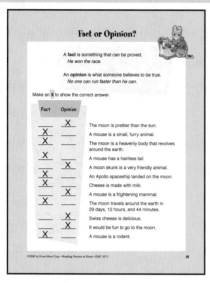

Fact or Opinion?

A **fact** is something that can be proved.
He won the race.

An **opinion** is what someone believes to be true.
No one can run faster than he can.

Make an **X** to show the correct answer.

Fact	Opinion	
	X	The moon is prettier than the sun.
X		A mouse is a small, furry animal.
X		The moon is a heavenly body that revolves around the earth.
X		A mouse has a hairless tail.
	X	A moon skunk is a very friendly animal.
X		An Apollo spaceship landed on the moon.
X		Cheese is made with milk.
	X	A mouse is a frightening mammal.
X		The moon travels around the earth in 29 days, 12 hours, and 44 minutes.
	X	Swiss cheese is delicious.
	X	It would be fun to go to the moon.
X		A mouse is a rodent.

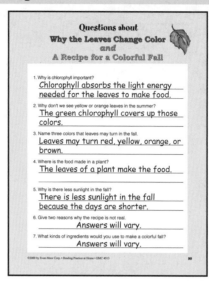

Questions about
Why the Leaves Change Color
and
A Recipe for a Colorful Fall

1. Why is chlorophyll important?
Chlorophyll absorbs the light energy needed for the leaves to make food.

2. Why don't we see yellow or orange leaves in the summer?
The green chlorophyll covers up those colors.

3. Name three colors that leaves may turn in the fall.
Leaves may turn red, yellow, orange, or brown.

4. Where is the food made in a plant?
The leaves of a plant make the food.

5. Why is there less sunlight in the fall?
There is less sunlight in the fall because the days are shorter.

6. Give two reasons why the recipe is not real.
Answers will vary.

7. What kinds of ingredients would you use to make a colorful fall?
Answers will vary.

Fact or Opinion?

A. Write **F** if the statement is a **fact** (something that is true).
Write **O** if the statement is an **opinion** (how someone feels or thinks).

O 1. Leaves are very beautiful in the fall.
F 2. The days are shorter in the fall.
O 3. Chilly nights are good for drinking hot chocolate.
F 4. Many leaves turn red, orange, and yellow in the fall.
O 5. It is nice to get a little rain in the fall.
O 6. Fall is my favorite season.
F 7. Leaves make the food for the plant.
F 8. Having less sunlight is why leaves start changing colors.
O 9. A harvest moon is what makes the fall season so pretty.
F 10. Lots of sunlight is needed to keep leaves green.

B. In the box below, draw a picture about fall.

Drawings will vary.

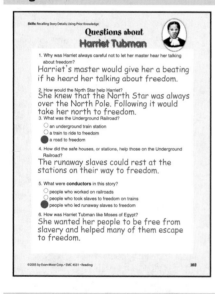

Skills: Recalling Story Details; Using Prior Knowledge

Questions about
Harriet Tubman

1. Why was Harriet always careful not to let her master hear her talking about freedom?
Harriet's master would give her a beating if he heard her talking about freedom.

2. How would the North Star help Harriet?
She knew that the North Star was always over the North Pole. Following it would take her north to freedom.

3. What was the Underground Railroad?
○ an underground train station
○ a train to ride to freedom
● a road to freedom

4. How did the safe houses, or stations, help those on the Underground Railroad?
The runaway slaves could rest at the stations on their way to freedom.

5. What were **conductors** in this story?
○ people who worked on railroads
○ people who took slaves to freedom on trains
● people who led runaway slaves to freedom

6. How was Harriet Tubman like Moses of Egypt?
She wanted her people to be free from slavery and helped many of them escape to freedom.

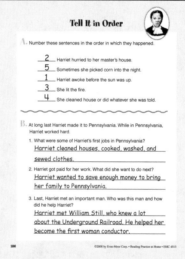

Tell It in Order

A. Number these sentences in the order in which they happened.

2 Harriet hurried to her master's house.
5 Sometimes she picked corn into the night.
1 Harriet awoke before the sun was up.
3 She lit the fire.
4 She cleaned house or did whatever she was told.

B. At long last Harriet made it to Pennsylvania. While in Pennsylvania, Harriet worked hard.

1. What were some of Harriet's first jobs in Pennsylvania?
Harriet cleaned houses, cooked, washed, and sewed clothes.

2. Harriet got paid for her work. What did she want to do next?
Harriet wanted to save enough money to bring her family to Pennsylvania.

3. Last, Harriet met an important man. Who was this man and how did he help Harriet?
Harriet met William Still, who knew a lot about the Underground Railroad. He helped her become the first woman conductor.

What Does It Mean?

Read the words in the box. Think about their meanings in the story of Harriet Tubman. Write each word next to its meaning.

slave	freedom	folks	patient
conductor	stations	master	cellar
underground	Egypt	border	Pharaoh

1. border — a dividing line between states or countries
2. stations — stopping places along a route or road
3. patient — able to wait for something
4. master — a person who has power over another
5. conductor — a person who guides or leads
6. freedom — not being controlled by others
7. Pharaoh — a king of old Egypt
8. underground — acting or doing something in secret
9. slave — a person owned by someone else
10. Egypt — a country in Africa
11. folks — people, or one's family or relatives
12. cellar — a room under a building where things are stored

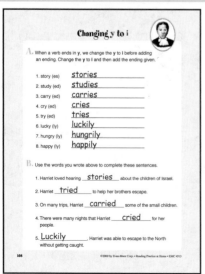

Changing y to i

A. When a verb ends in y, we change the y to i before adding an ending. Change the y to i and then add the ending given.

1. story (es) stories
2. study (ed) studies
3. carry (ed) carries
4. cry (ed) cries
5. try (ed) tries
6. lucky (ly) luckily
7. hungry (ly) hungrily
8. happy (ly) happily

B. Use the words you wrote above to complete these sentences.

1. Harriet loved hearing stories about the children of Israel.
2. Harriet tried to help her brothers escape.
3. On many trips, Harriet carried some of the small children.
4. There were many nights that Harriet cried for her people.
5. Luckily, Harriet was able to escape to the North without getting caught.

Skills: Understanding and Using Contractions

Contractions

A contraction is a shortened form of a pair of words.

A. Write the words that each contraction stands for. Circle the letter or letters that were left out when the contraction was made.

1. it's — it is
2. she's — she is
3. that's — that is
4. he's — he is
5. I'll — I will
6. we'll — we will
7. she'll — she will
8. he'll — he will
9. wasn't — was not
10. isn't — is not
11. shouldn't — should not
12. couldn't — could not

B. Write sentences using four of the contractions above.
1. Sentences will vary.
2.
3.
4.

C. Write the contraction for these words.
1. she is — she's
2. was not — wasn't
3. we will — we'll
4. that is — that's

Follow the North Star

The story said that the slaves used the North Star to guide them north to freedom. The North Star is easy to find if you first find the Big Dipper constellation. The two stars at the outer edge of the cup point to the North Star.

Use the drawing below. Go outside on a clear night and try to find the North Star.*

spring
summer
Polaris
(North Star)
autumn
winter

Answers will vary.

☐ I found the North Star.

*You can only do this if you live in the Northern Hemisphere.